easy piano

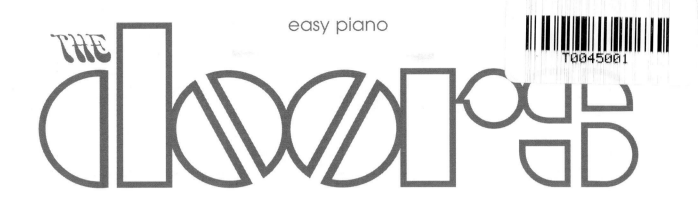

ISBN 978-0-634-00469-8

HAL•LEONARD®
CORPORATION

7777 W. BLUEMOUND RD. P.O. BOX 13819 MILWAUKEE, WI 53213

Visit Hal Leonard Online at
www.halleonard.com

In the studio
© Doors Photo Archive

THE DOORS

CONTENTS

5	Break on Through (To the Other Side)
10	The End
20	Five to One
25	Hello, I Love You
30	L.A. Woman
46	Light My Fire
50	Love Her Madly
39	Love Me Two Times
56	People Are Strange
62	Riders on the Storm
66	Strange Days
80	Touch Me
86	The Unknown Soldier
73	When the Music's Over
90	You Make Me Real

Soundstage TV performance
© Doors Photo Archive

BREAK ON THROUGH
(To the Other Side)

Words and Music by
JIM MORRISON

With a quick beat

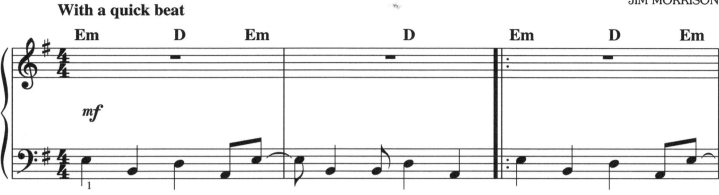

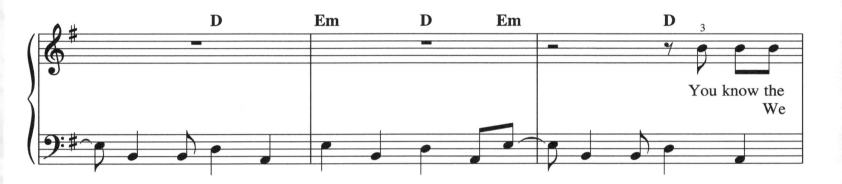

You know the
We

day de- stroys the night, ___
chased our pleas- ures here, ___
is- land in your arms, ___

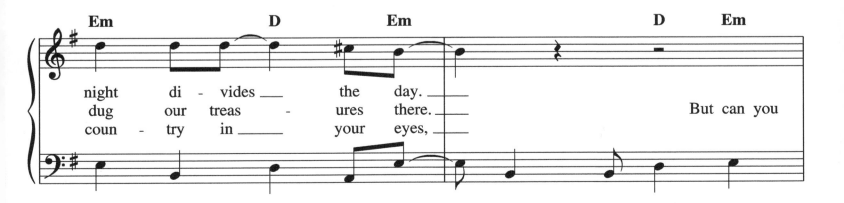

night di- vides ___ the day. ___
dug our treas- ures there. ___
coun- try in ___ your eyes, ___

But can you

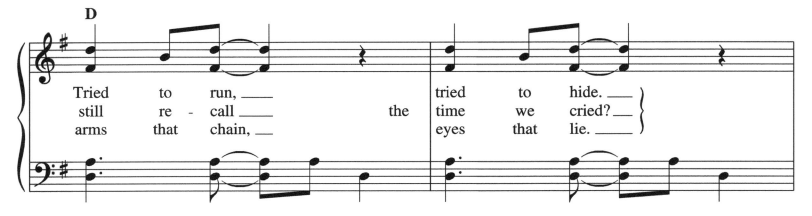

Tried to run, _____ tried to hide. _____
still re - call _____ the time we cried? ___
arms that chain, _____ eyes that lie. _____

Break on through _ to the oth - er side, _ break on through _ to the

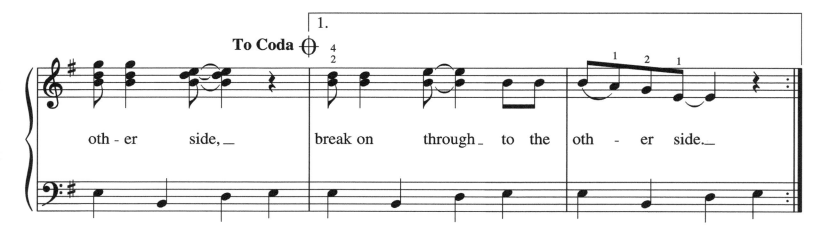

oth - er side, _ break on through _ to the oth - er side. _

(Instrumental)

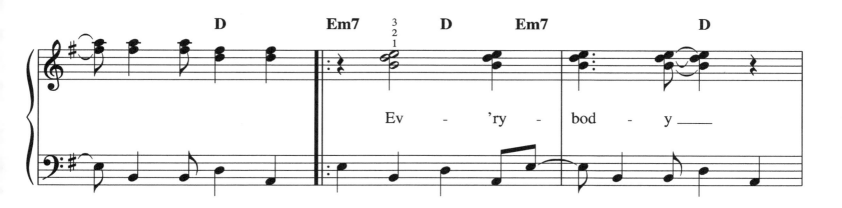

Ev - 'ry - bod - y ____

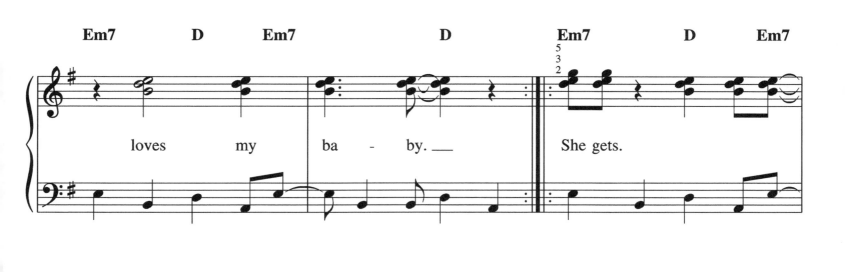

loves my ba - by. ____   She gets.

8

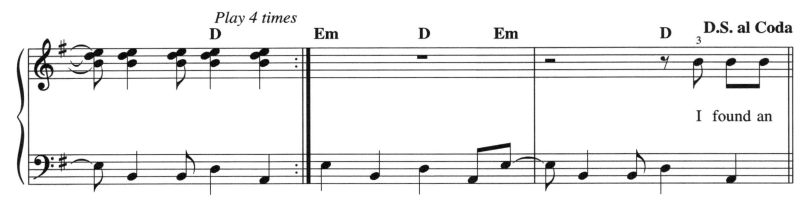

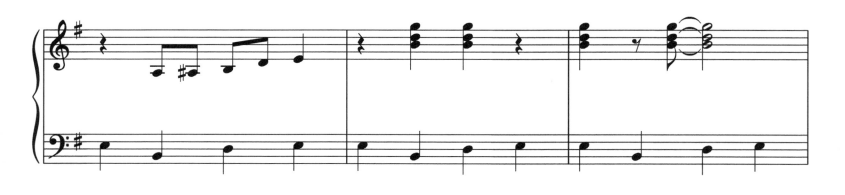

week to week,_   day to day, _   hour to hour. _   The

D   **Em7**

gate is straight, _   deep and wide._   Break on   through _ to the

oth - er   side. _   Break on   through, _   break on   through. _

Break,   break,   break,   break,   break.

THE END

Words and Music by
THE DOORS

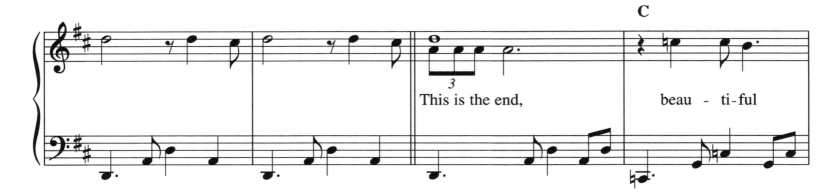

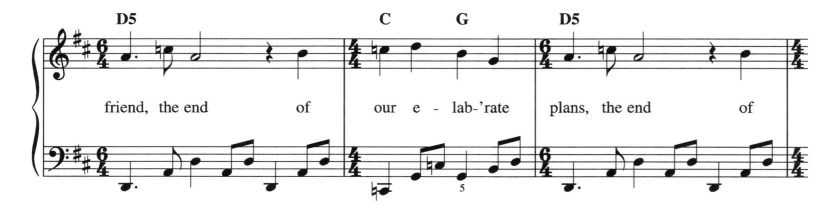

ev - 'ry - thing that stands, the end. No safe - ty or sur -

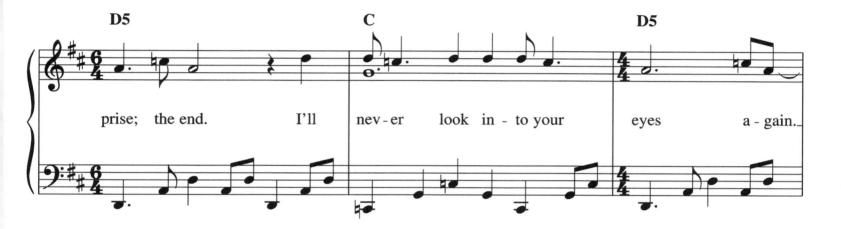

prise; the end. I'll nev - er look in - to your eyes a - gain.

_____ Can you pic - ture ___ what will

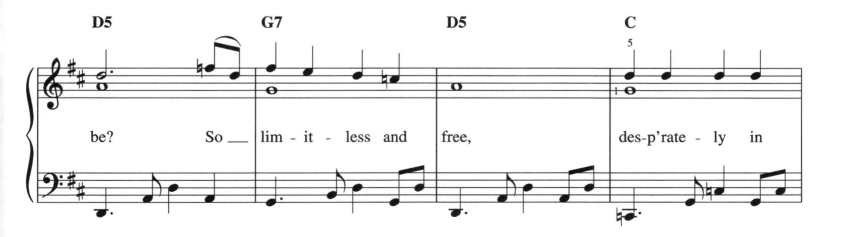

be? So ___ lim - it - less and free, des - p'rate - ly in

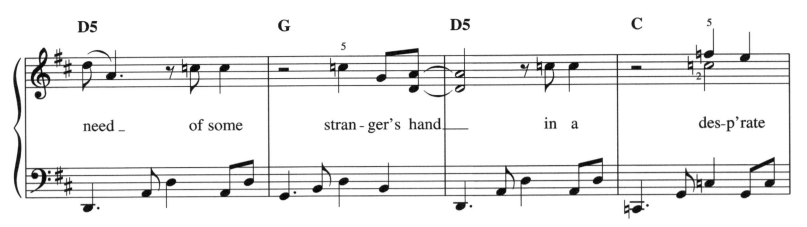

need _ of some stran - ger's hand _ in a des-p'rate

land.

Lost in a Ro-man wil - der - ness of pain,

_ and

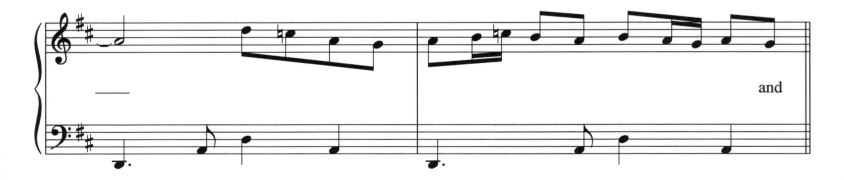

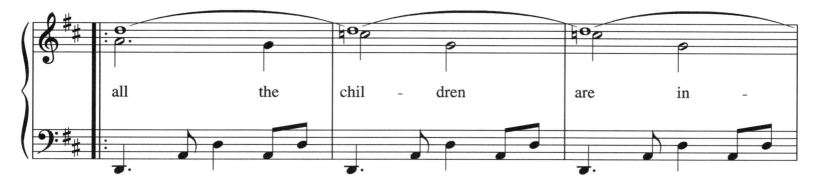

all   the   chil - dren   are   in -

sane.   Wait-ing   for   the

sum-mer   rain, _____   yeah. _____   There's

dan - ger _____   on   the   edge of ___ town. _

Ride the king's high - way. _____

Weird scenes in - side _____

_____ the gold _ mine.

Ride the high - way west, _____ ba - by.

He's old, ___

and his   skin is   cold. _

The West   is the best._

The

West is the best. ____

Get here, and we'll do the rest.

The blue bus ____ is call - ing us.

1.

2.

Driv - er, where you

tak - ing us? __

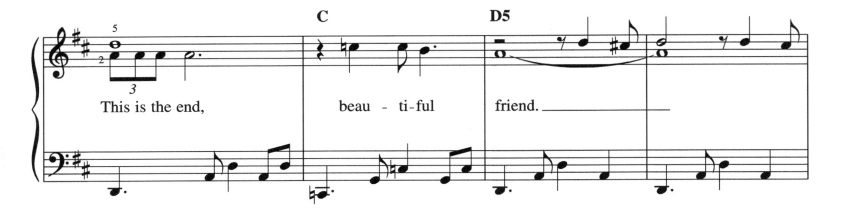

C   **D5**

This is the end,   beau - ti-ful   friend. _____

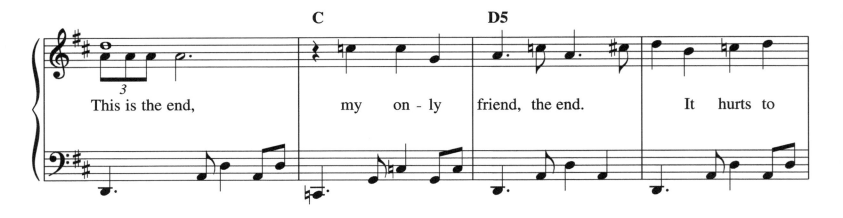

C   **D5**

This is the end,   my   on - ly   friend, the end.   It   hurts to

set you   free, __   but you'll   nev - er   fol - low   me. _____

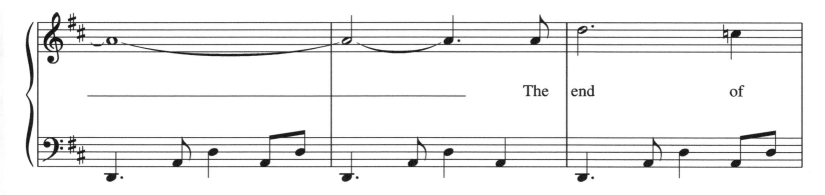

The end of

laugh - ter and soft lies. The

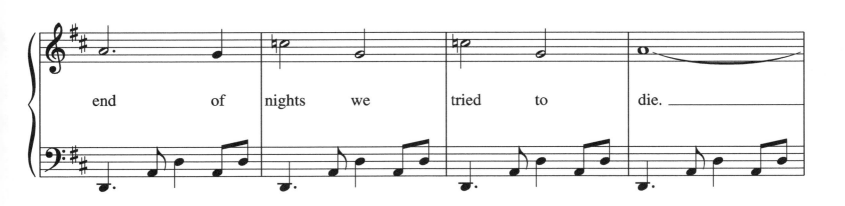

end of nights we tried to die.

This is the end.

rit.

FIVE TO ONE

Words and Music by
THE DOORS

Slow and heavy

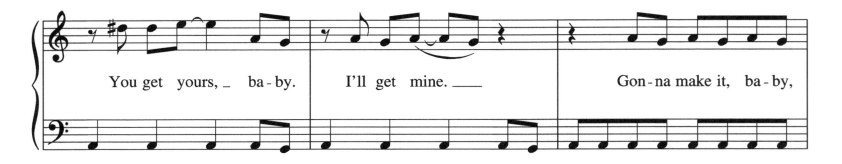

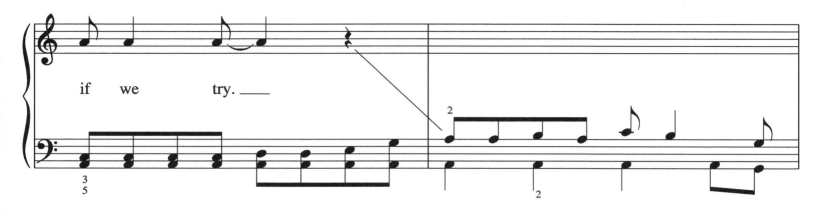

if we try. ___

The old get old ___ and the young get strong - er.

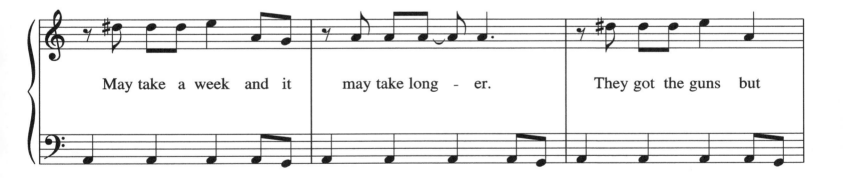

May take a week and it may take long - er. They got the guns but

N.C.

we got the num-bers. Gon-na win, _ yeah, we're tak-in' o - ver.

Come on!

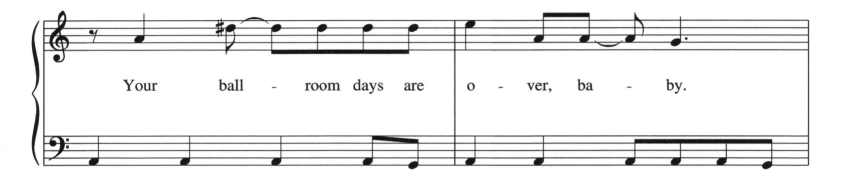

Your ball - room days are o - ver, ba - by.

Night is draw - ing near. __ Shad-ows __ of the

eve - ning __ crawl a - cross the years. _____

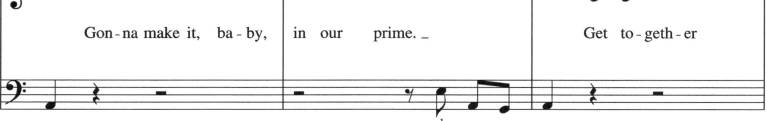

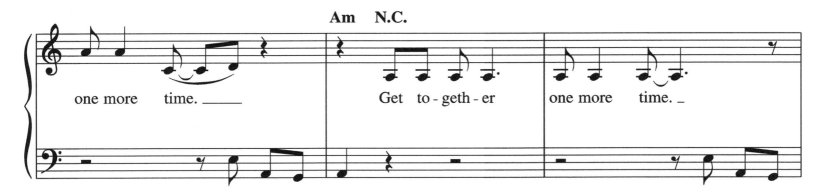

one more time. _____   Get to-geth-er   one more time. _

Get to-geth-er   one more time. _   Get to-geth-er

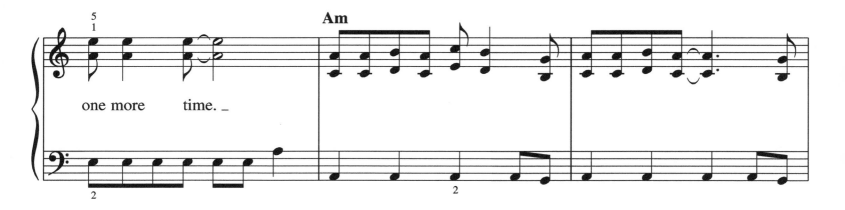

one more time. _

HELLO, I LOVE YOU
(WON'T YOU TELL ME YOUR NAME?)

Words and Music by
THE DOORS

Medium Rock beat

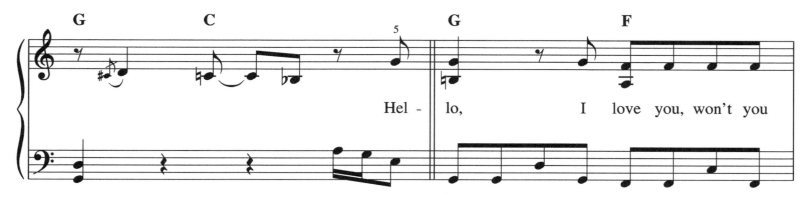

Hel - lo,   I   love you, won't you

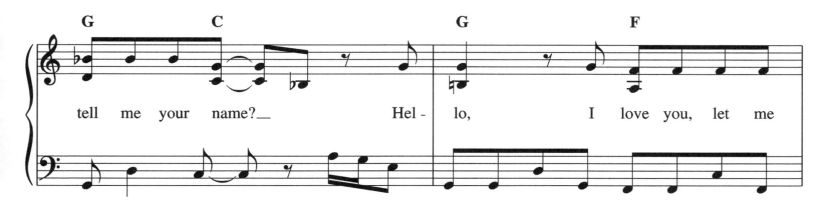

tell me your name?__   Hel - lo,   I   love you, let me

jump in your game. __   Hel - lo,   I   love you, won't you

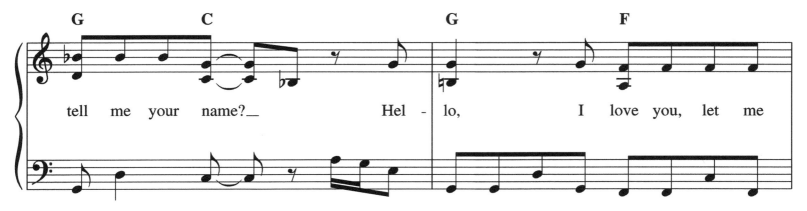

tell me your name?__ Hel - lo, I love you, let me

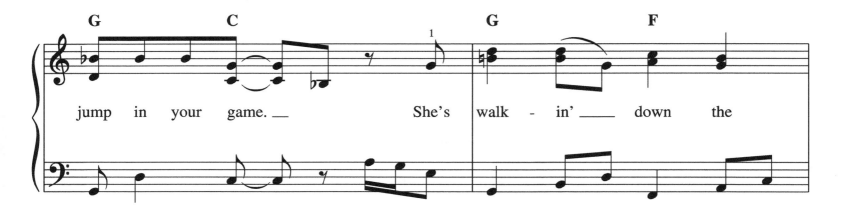

jump in your game. __ She's walk - in' ____ down the

street, _____ blind to ___ ev - 'ry eye she meets.__ Do you

think you'll _ be the guy _____ to make the _ queen of the

an - gels sigh?__ Hel - lo, I love you, won't you

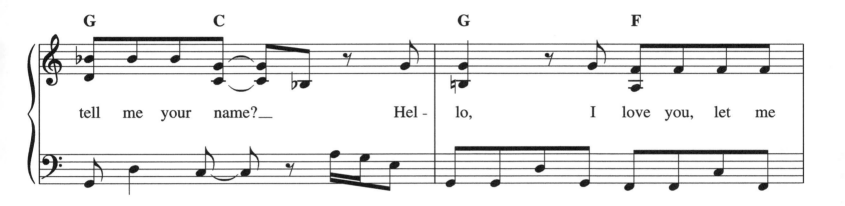

tell me your name?__ Hel - lo, I love you, let me

jump in your game. __ Hel - lo, I love you, won't you

tell me your name?__ Hel - lo, I love you, let me

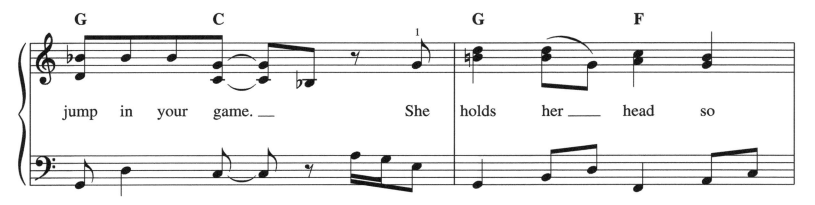

jump in your game. ___ She holds her ___ head so

high, _____ like a stat - ue ___ in the sky. _____ Her

arms are __ wick-ed and her legs are long. _ When she moves, my brain screams

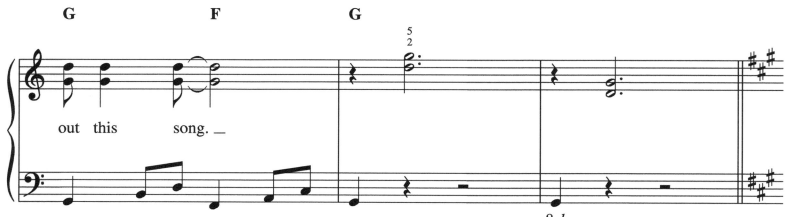

out this song. _

L.A. WOMAN

Words and Music by
THE DOORS

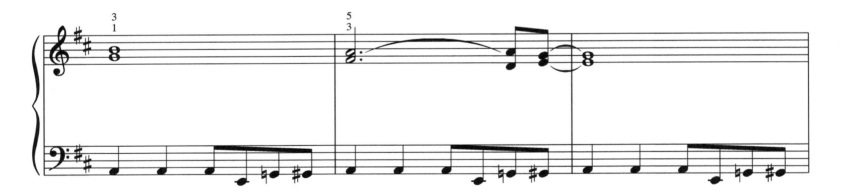

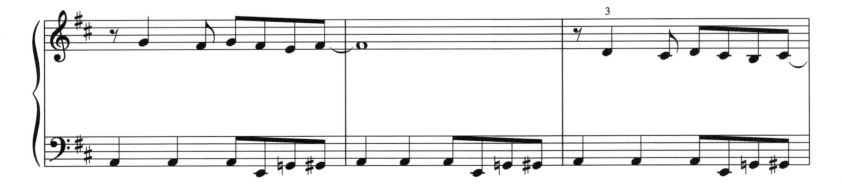

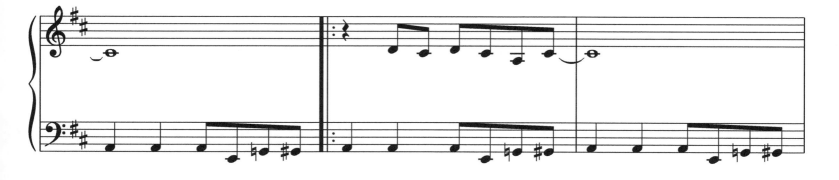

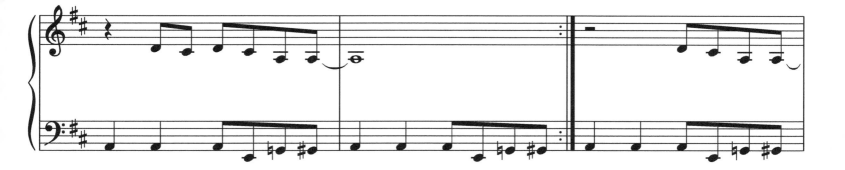

Well, I just got in - to town a - bout an

hour a - go. ___   I

took a look a-round, see which____ way the wind_ blow,

with a lit - tle girl in a Hol - ly-wood bun - ga - low.__

Are you a luck - y lit - tle la - dy in the

cit - y of light, _ or just an -

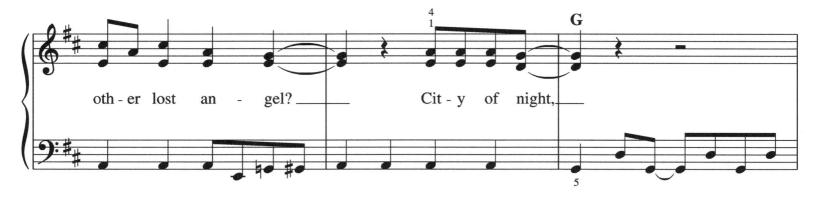

oth - er lost an - gel? _____ Cit - y of night, _____

cit - y of night, _____ cit - y of night, _____

To Coda

cit - y of night. _____

L. A.__ wom - an,   L. A.__ wom - an;

L. A.   wom - an, Sun-day   af - ter - noon,__

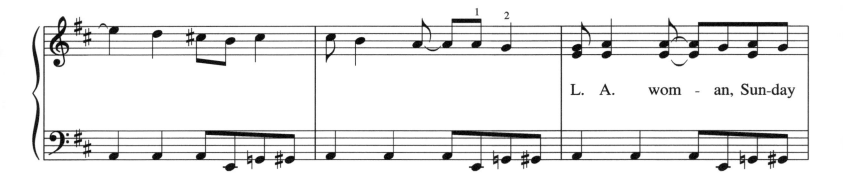

L. A.   wom - an, Sun-day

af - ter - noon.__

L. A.   wom - an, Sun-day   af - ter - noon,_   drive through your sub-urbs

in - to your   blues,   in - to your

A

blues,   yeah,   in - to your   blue,   blue,_   blue,_

A

_   in - to your   blues.

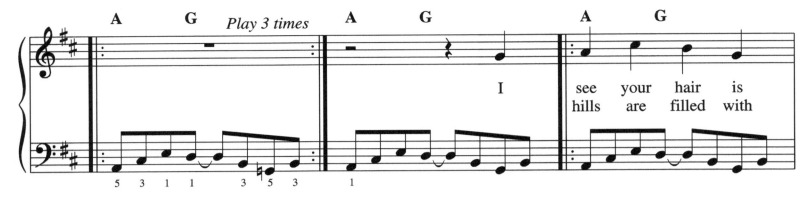

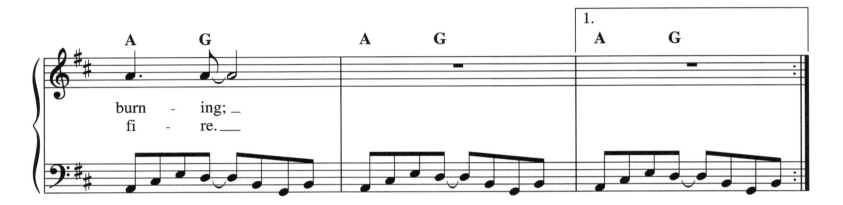

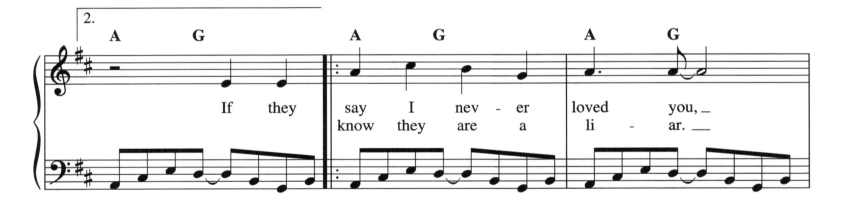

Driv - in' down your free - way, __
mid - night al - leys roam;

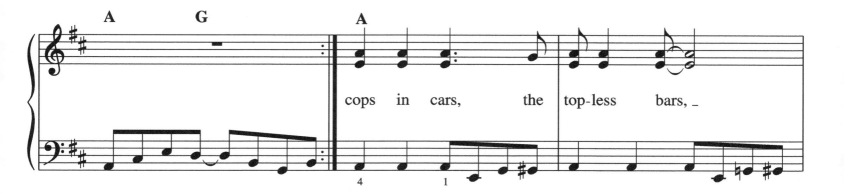

cops in cars, the top-less bars, __

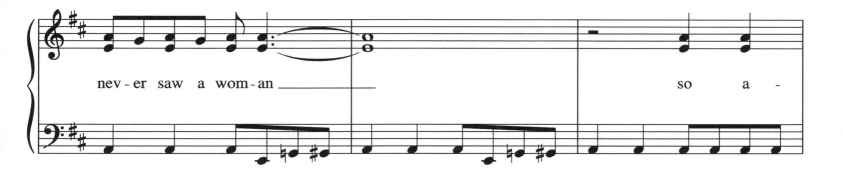

nev - er saw a wom-an __ so a -

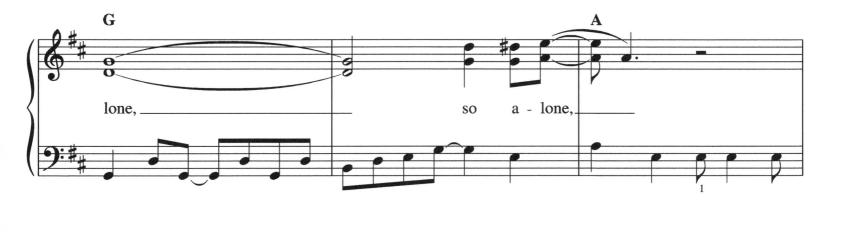

lone, __ so a - lone, __

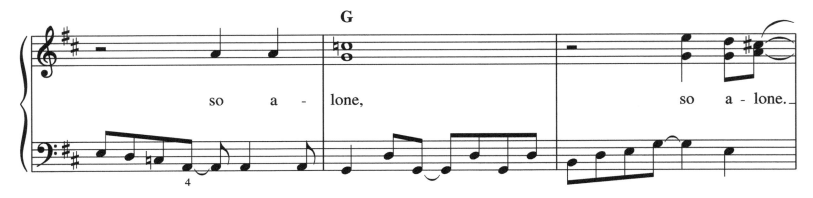

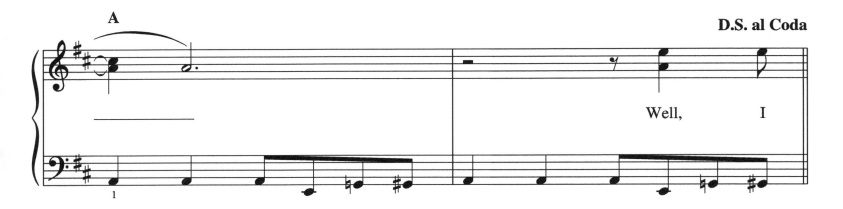

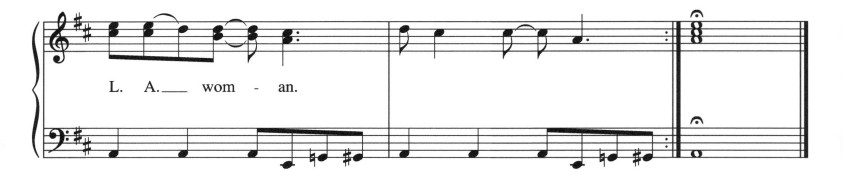

LOVE ME TWO TIMES

Words and Music by
THE DOORS

Hard Blues

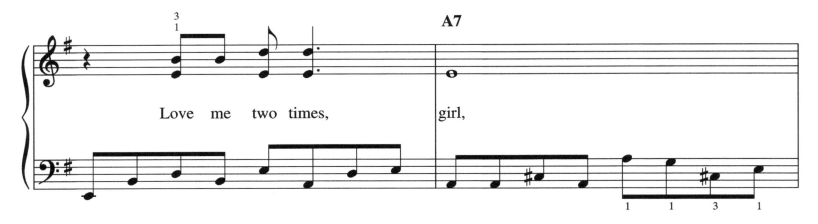

Love me two times, girl,

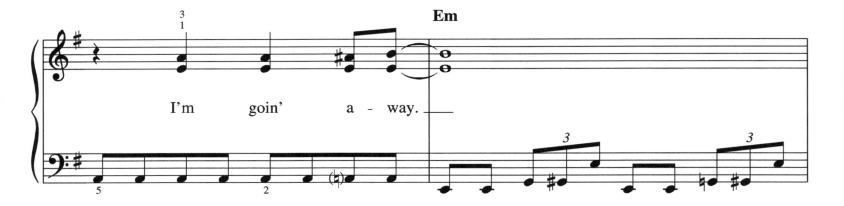

I'm goin' a - way.

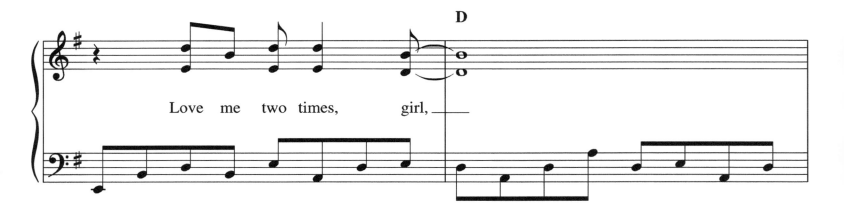

Love me two times, girl,

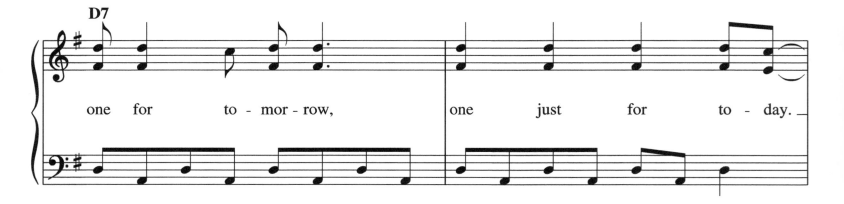

one for to - mor - row, one just for to - day.

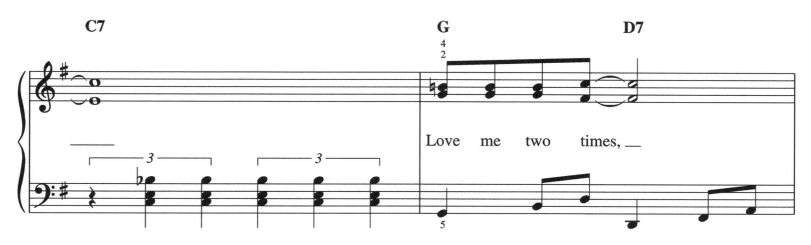

Love me two **times**, ___

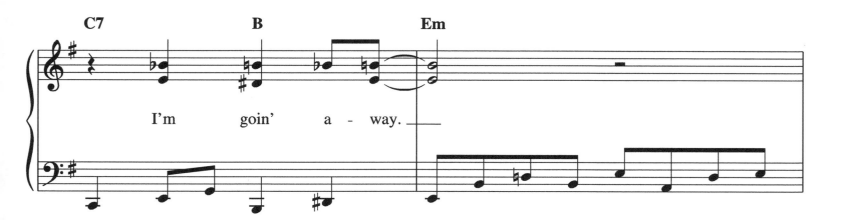

I'm goin' a - way. ___

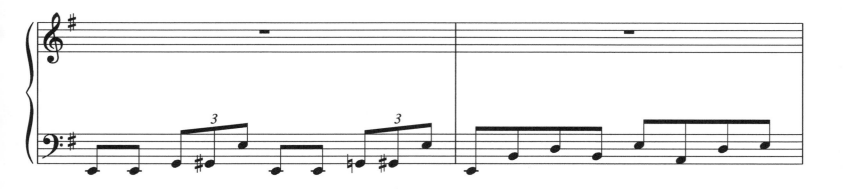

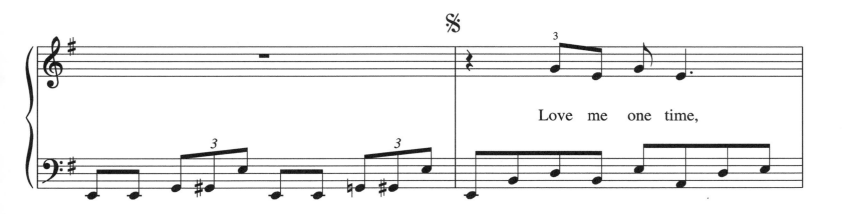

Love me one time,

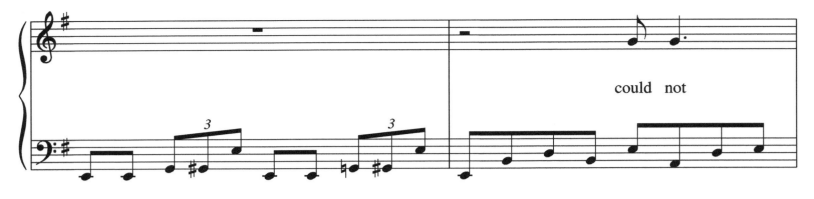

could not

speak.

Love me one time,

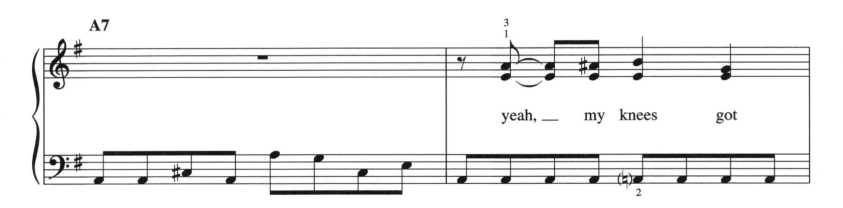

A7

yeah, __ my knees got

Em

weak.

Love me two times, girl, __

43

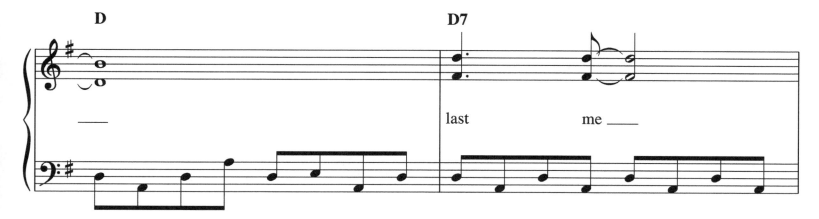

last   me _____

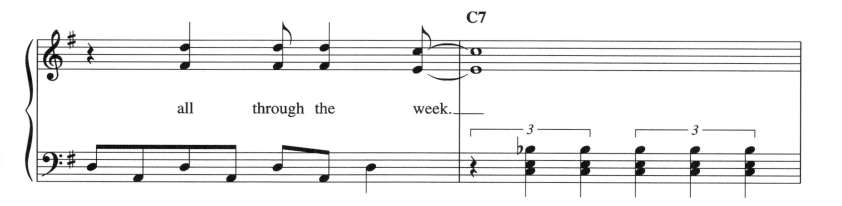

all   through the   week. _____

To Coda

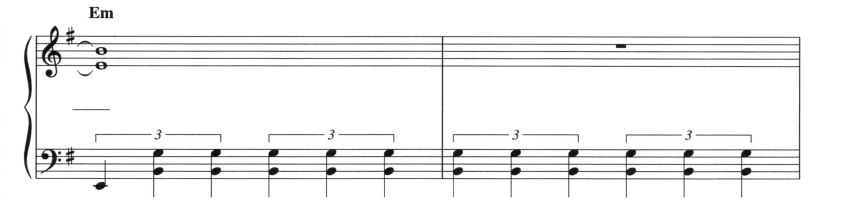

Love me two times, _   I'm   goin'   a - way. _

44

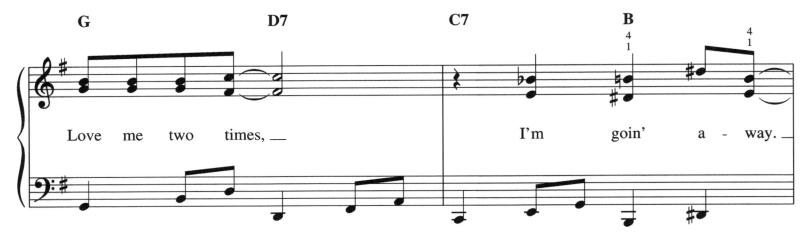

Love me two times, ___ I'm goin' a - way.

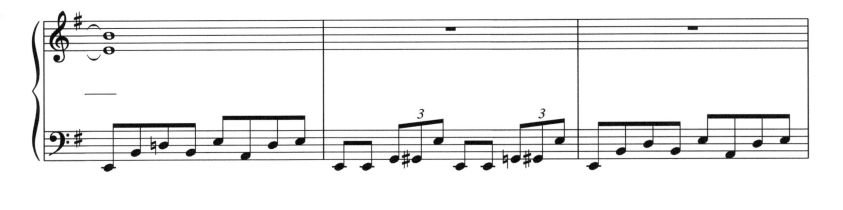

D.S. al Coda

CODA **C7** **B**

I'm goin' a - way. ___

Em

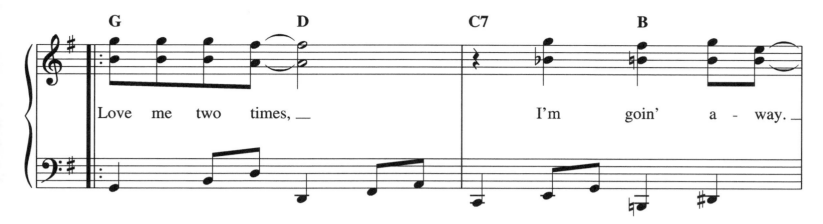

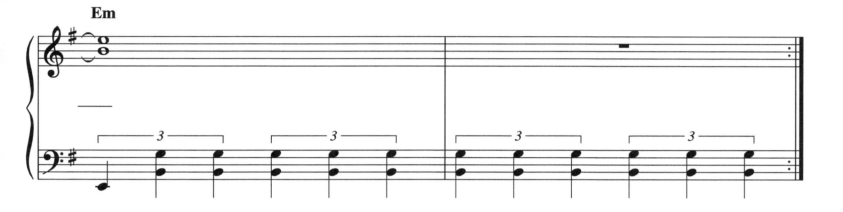

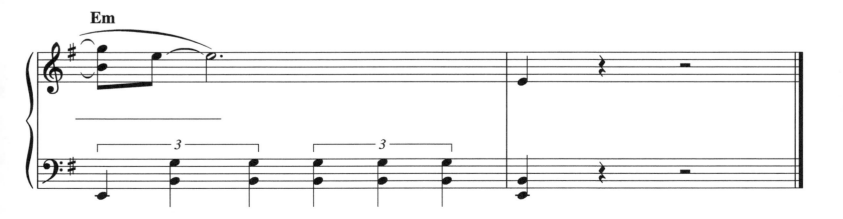

LIGHT MY FIRE

Words and Music by
THE DOORS

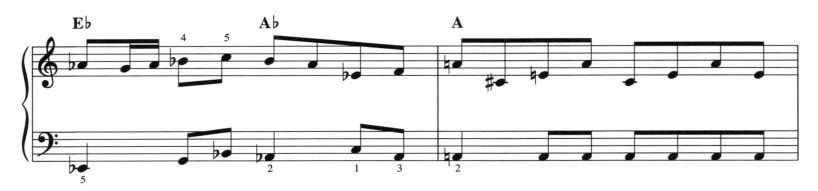

You know that it would be un-true,____
time to hes-i-tate is through;

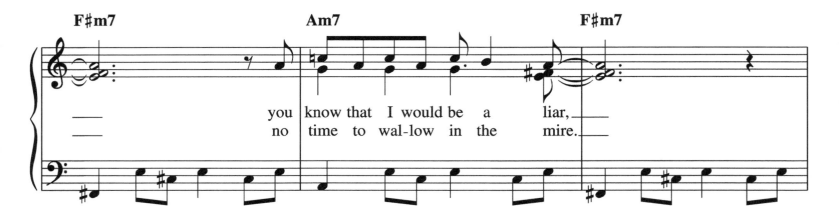

____ you know that I would be a liar,____
____ no time to wal-low in the mire.____

if I was to say to you,____ girl, we could-n't get much higher.
Try now, we can on - ly lose,____ and our love be-come a fun - 'ral pyre.

Come on, ba - by, light my fire.____

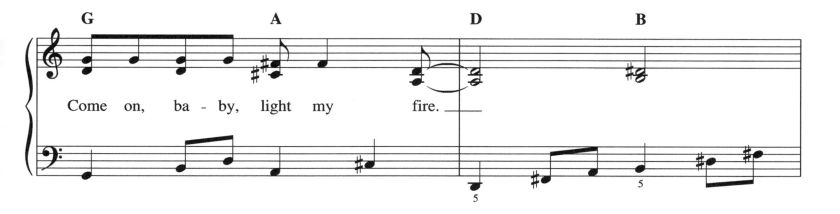

Come on, ba - by, light my fire.____

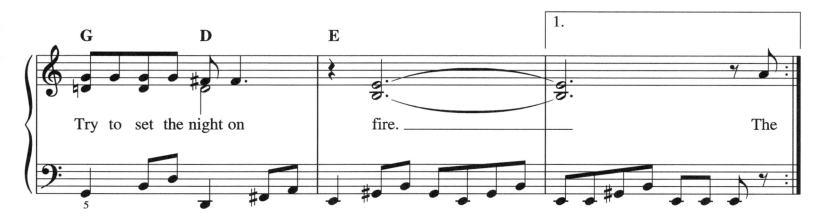

Try to set the night on fire.____

1.

The

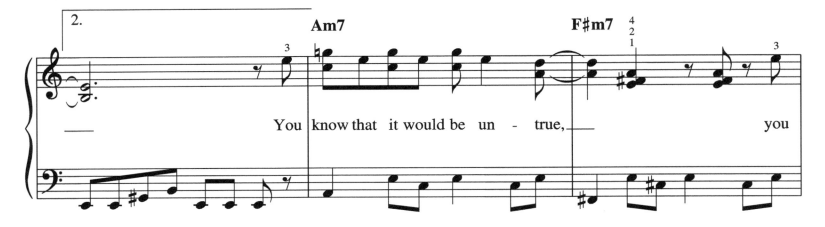

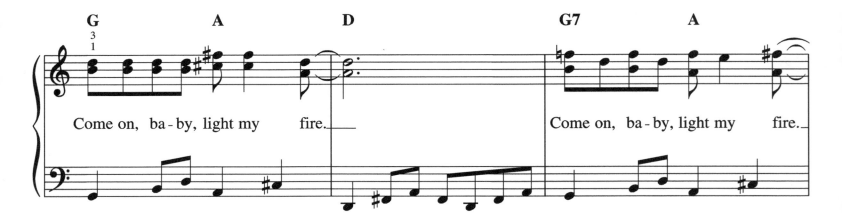

Play 3 times

Try to set the night on fire.

Try to set the night on fire.

L.H.

R.H.

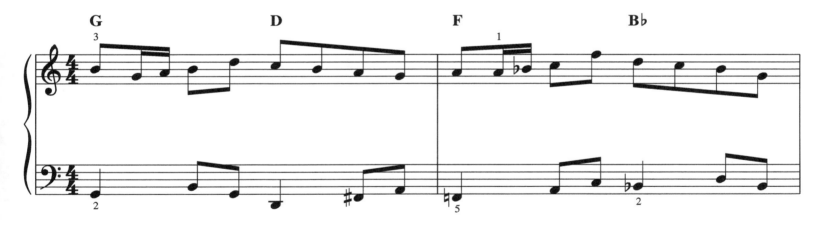

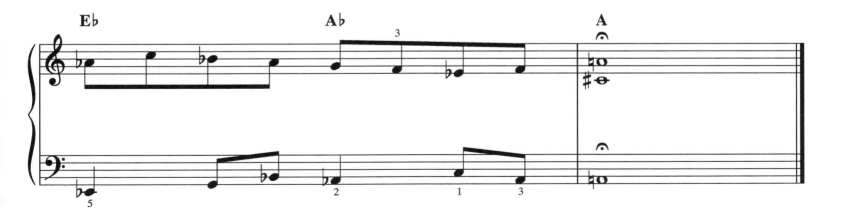

LOVE HER MADLY

Words and Music by
THE DOORS

Don't you love her mad - ly? Want to

be her dad - dy? Don't you love her___ face?___

Don't you love her as___ she's walk - ing out___ the door,

___ like she did ___ one

thou - sand times be - fore? ___ Don't you

love her ways? _ Tell me what you say. __

Don't you love her as ___ she's walk - ing out the door? _

All your love, __

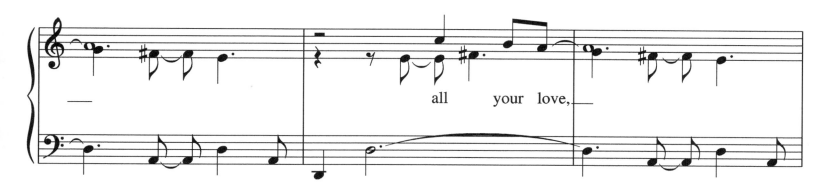

all your love,___ all your

love, all your love is ___ gone,_ so sing a

lone - ly song _ of a deep blue dream._

To Coda

Sev - en   hors - es   seem __   to   be   on   the

mark. _____

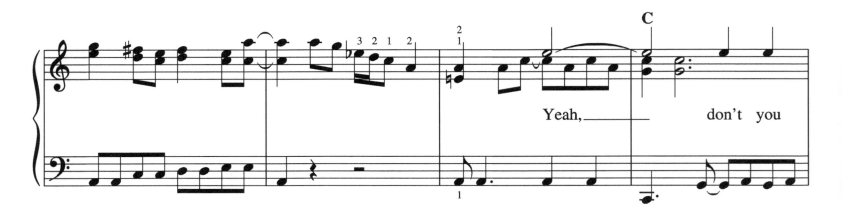

Yeah, _____   don't   you

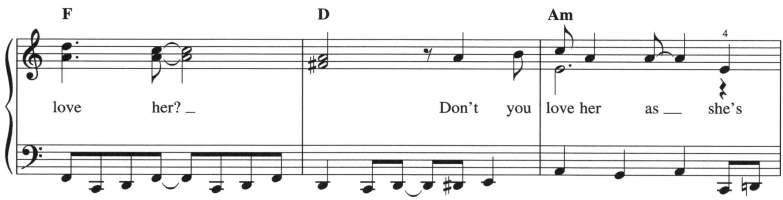

love her? _ Don't you love her as __ she's

walk - ing out __ the door? __

D.S. al Coda

CODA

Well, don't you love her mad - ly?

Oh, don't you love her mad - ly?

PEOPLE ARE STRANGE

Words and Music by
THE DOORS

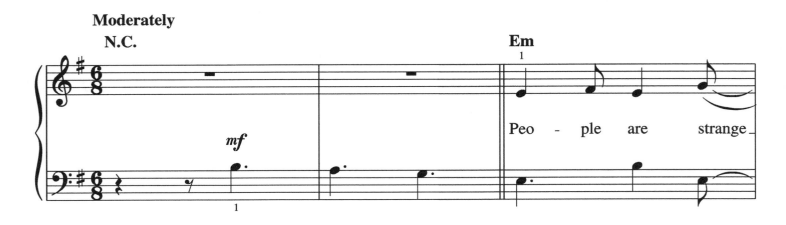

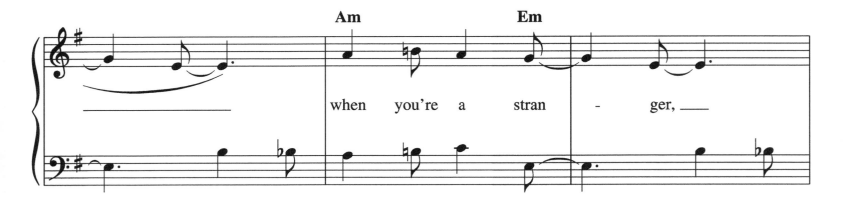

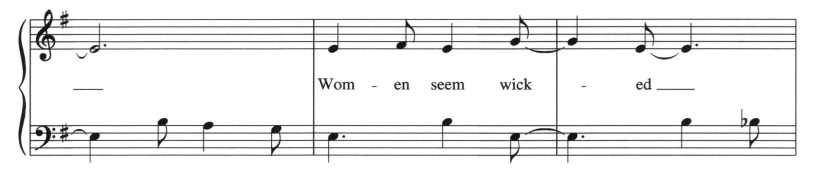

57

58

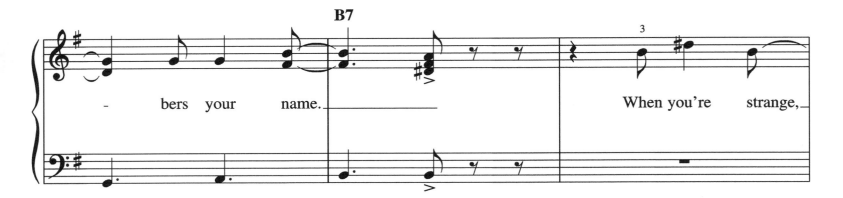

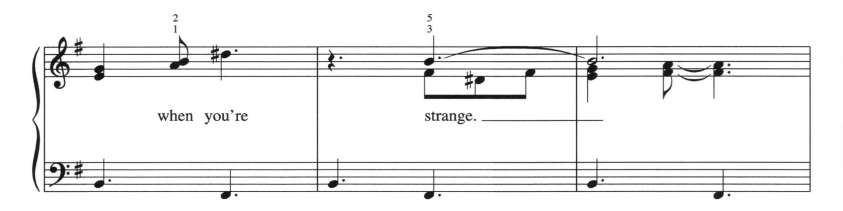

Peo - ple are strange

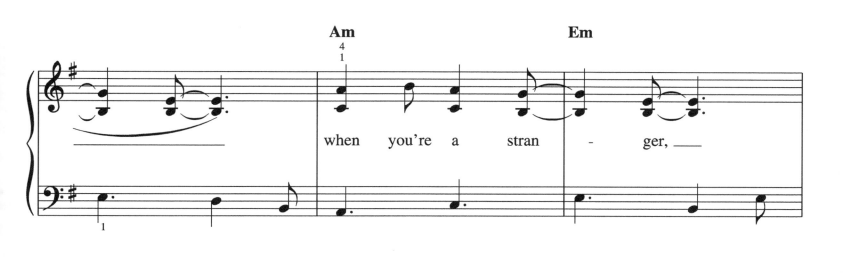

when you're a stran - ger, ____

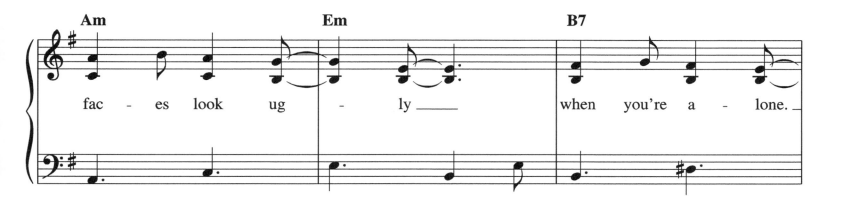

fac - es look ug - ly ____ when you're a - lone.

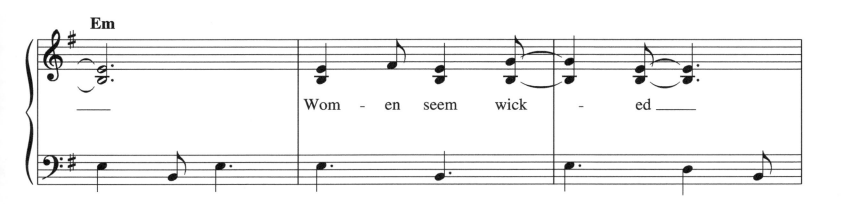

Wom - en seem wick - ed ____

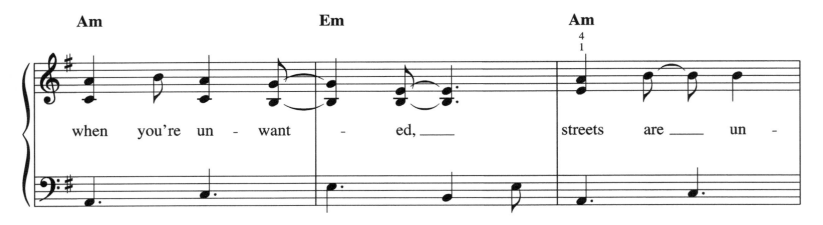

when   you're un - want - ed, ___   streets   are ___   un -

e - ven ___   when you're   down. ___

D.S. al Coda

When you're

CODA

when you're   strange.

RIDERS ON THE STORM

Words and Music by
THE DOORS

Easy Rock

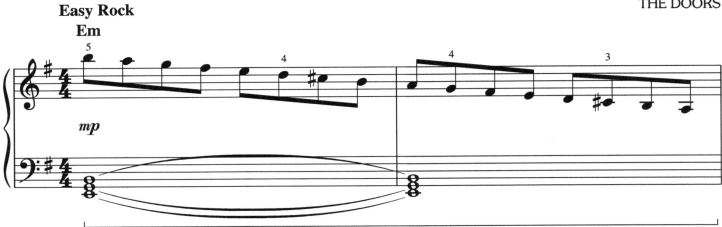

Rid-ers on the storm.____

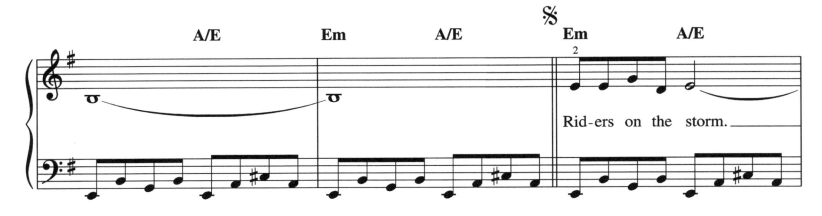

Rid-ers on the storm._____ In -

to this house we're born.   In - to this world we're thrown.____

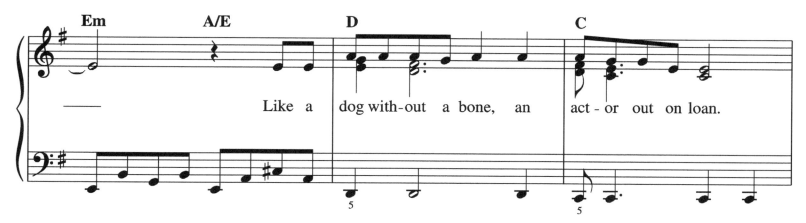

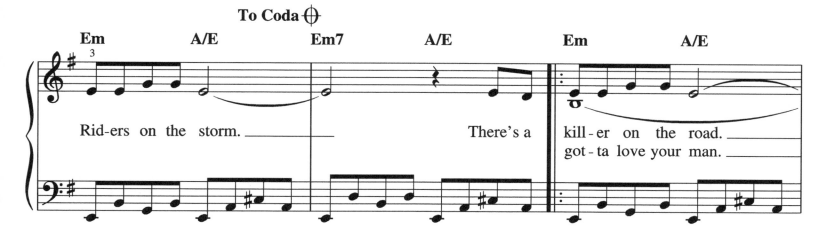

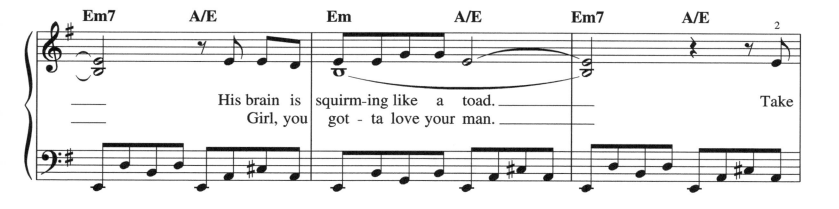

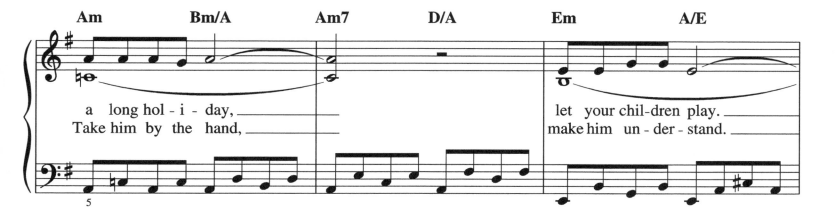

64

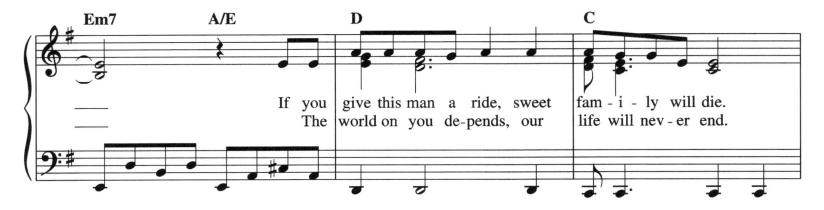

If you give this man a ride, sweet fam - i - ly will die.
The world on you de-pends, our life will nev - er end.

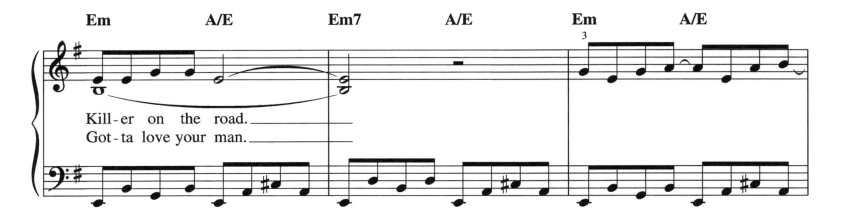

Kill-er on the road.
Got-ta love your man.

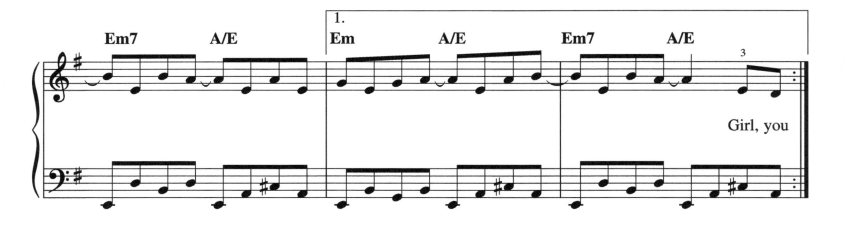

Girl, you

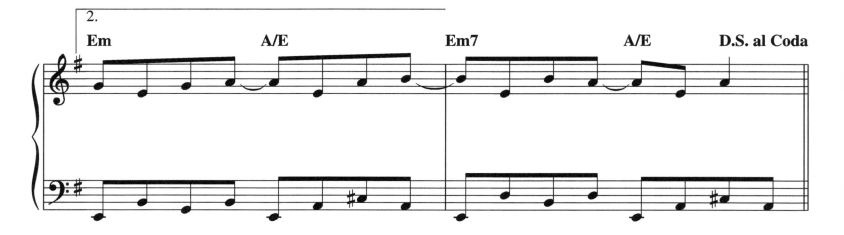

D.S. al Coda

CODA

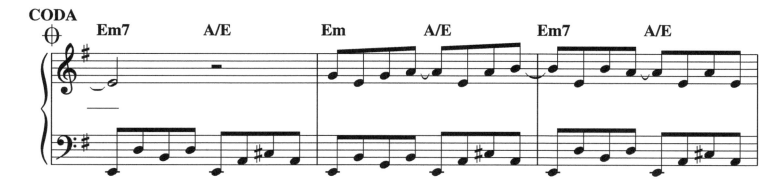

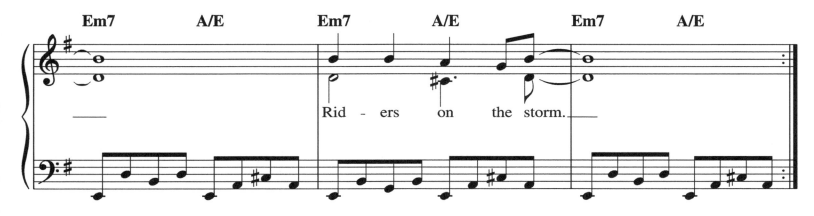

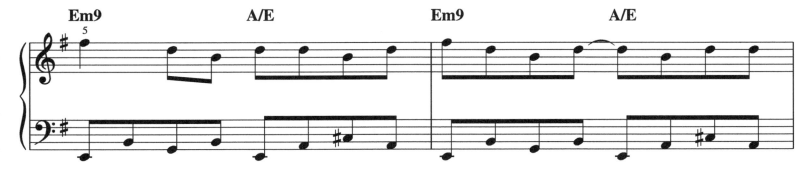

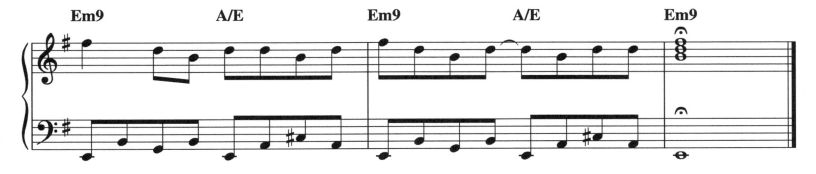

STRANGE DAYS

Words and Music by
THE DOORS

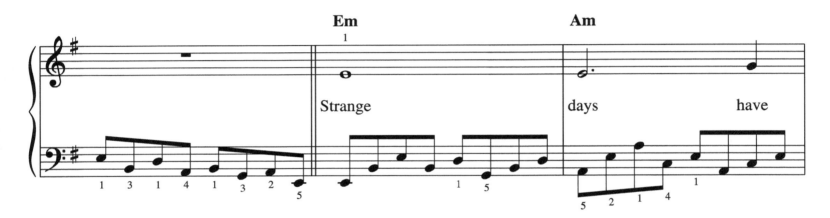

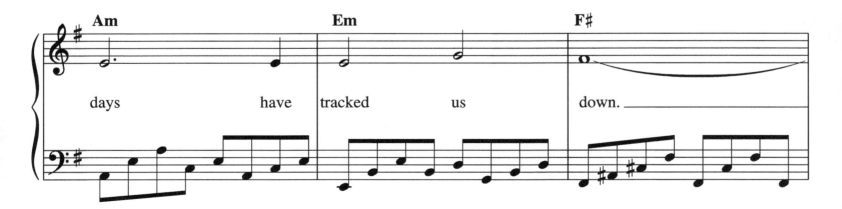

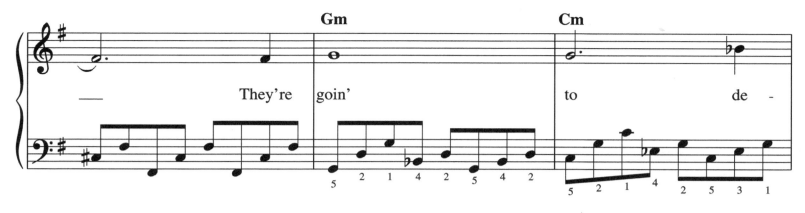

They're goin' to de-

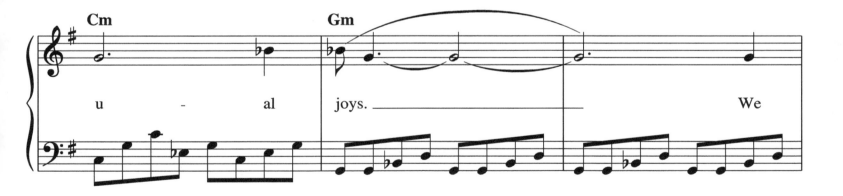

stroy _____ our cas-

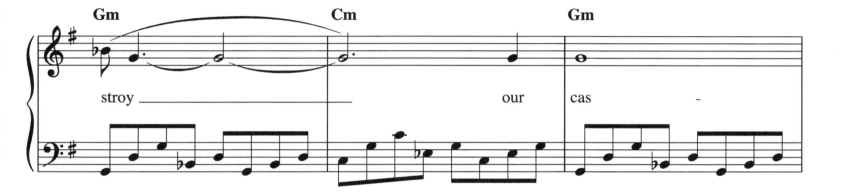

u - al joys. _____ We

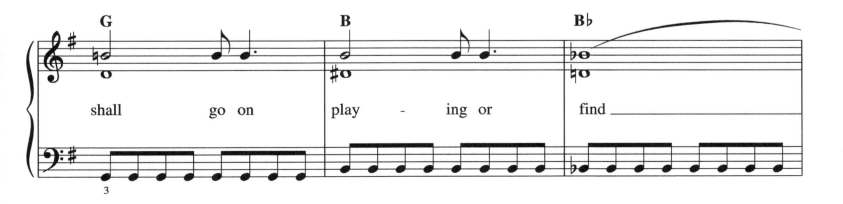

shall go on play - ing or find _____

a new town.

Play 3 times

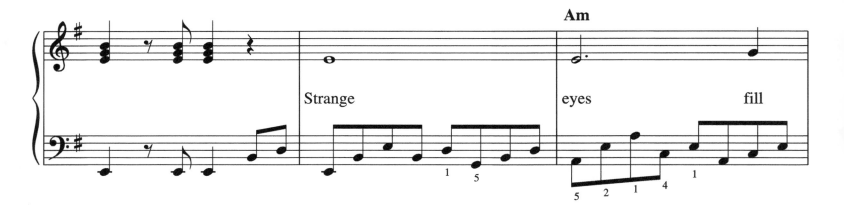

Strange eyes fill

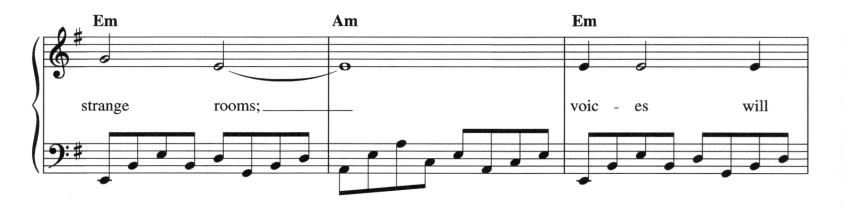

strange rooms; voic - es will

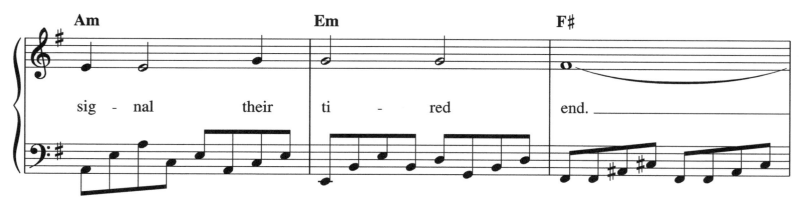

sig - nal their ti - red end. _____

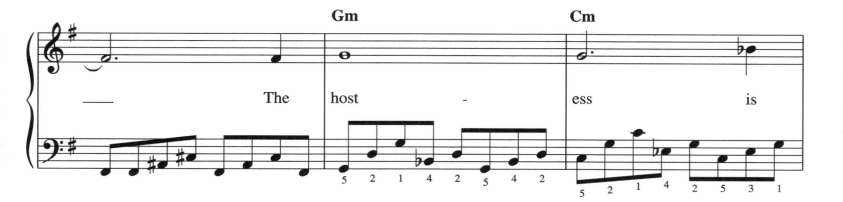

_____ The host - ess is

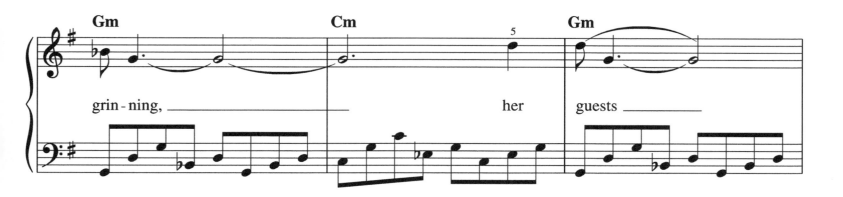

grin - ning, _____ her guests _____

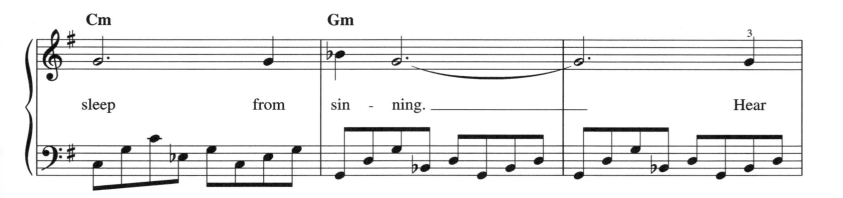

sleep from sin - ning. _____ Hear

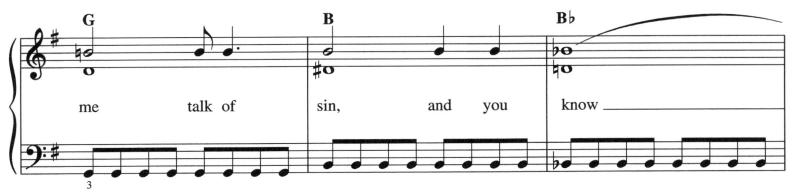

me · talk of · sin, · and · you · know _____

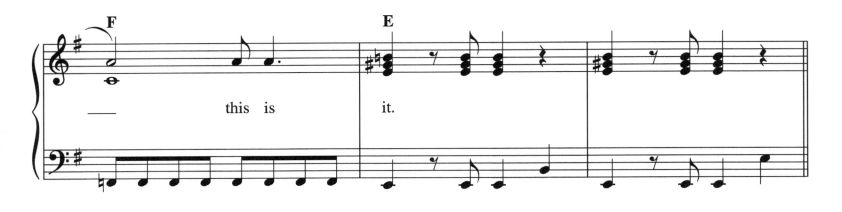

_____ · this · is · it.

Play 3 times

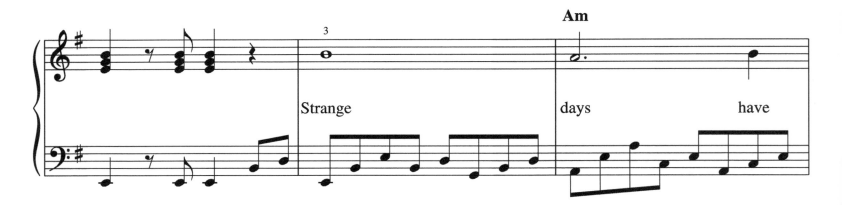

Strange · days · have

found us, _____ and through their strange

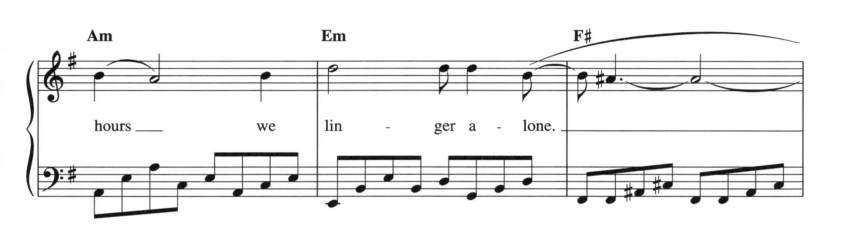

hours _____ we lin - ger a - lone. _____

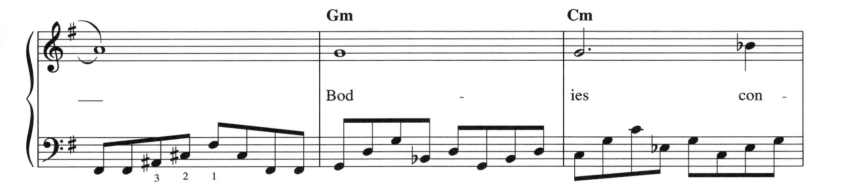

_____ Bod - ies con -

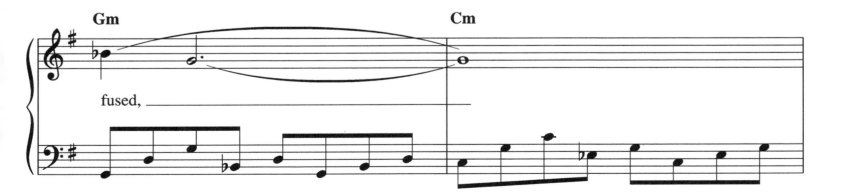

fused, _____

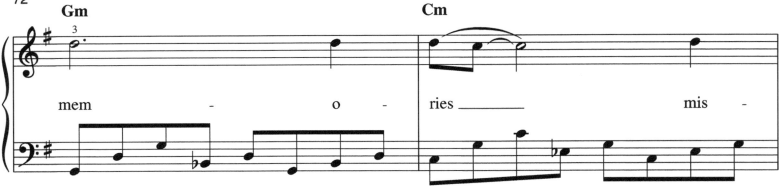

mem - o - ries _____ mis -

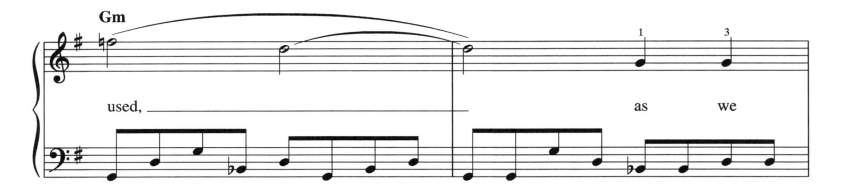

used, _____ as we

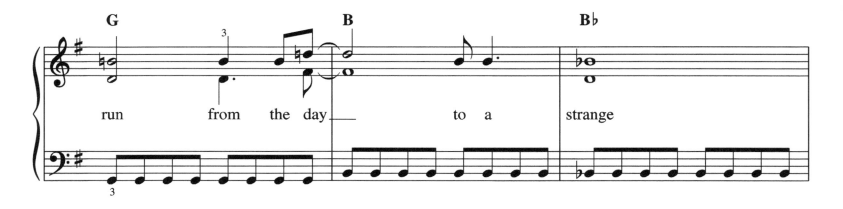

run from the day___ to a strange

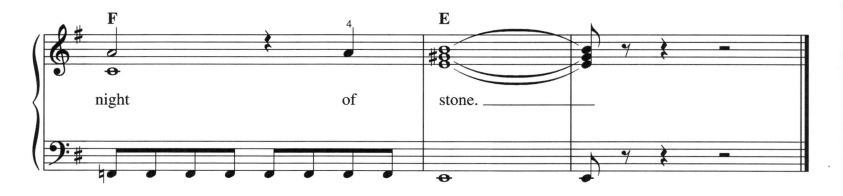

night of stone. _____

WHEN THE MUSIC'S OVER

Words and Music by
THE DOORS

Moderate Blues

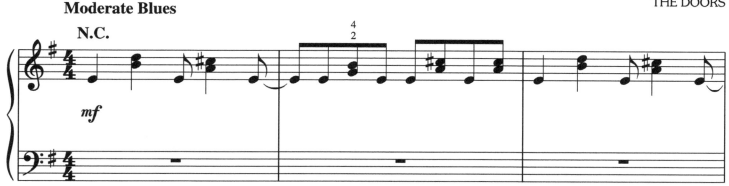

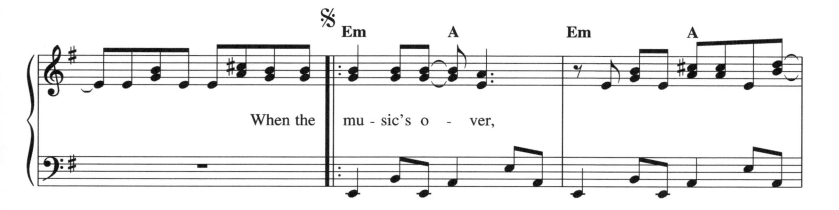

mu - sic's o - ver, turn out the lights, ___ turn out the lights, ___

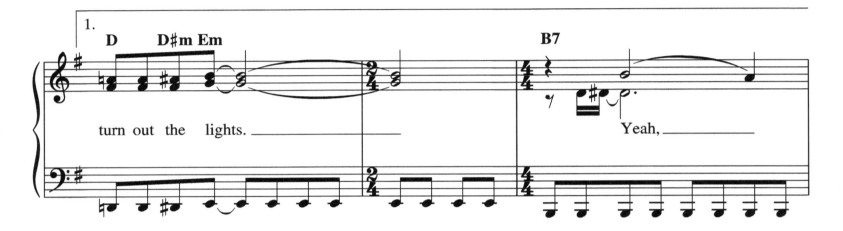

1.

turn out the lights. ___ Yeah, ___

yeah. ___

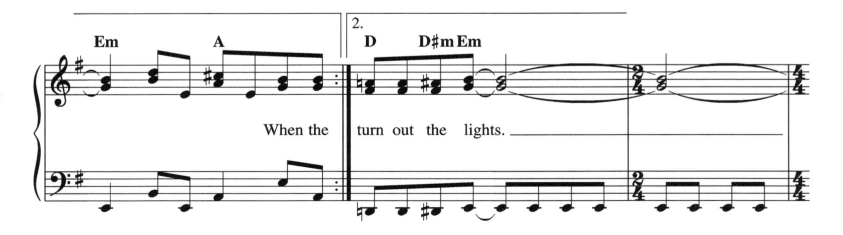

2.

When the turn out the lights. ___

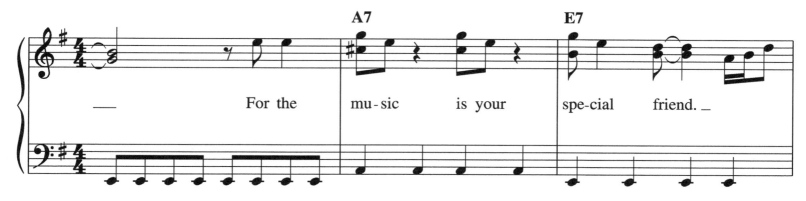

For the mu-sic is your spe-cial friend. _

Dance _ on fire _ as it in - tends. _ Mu-sic is your

on - ly friend _ un -

til the end, _ un - til the end, _

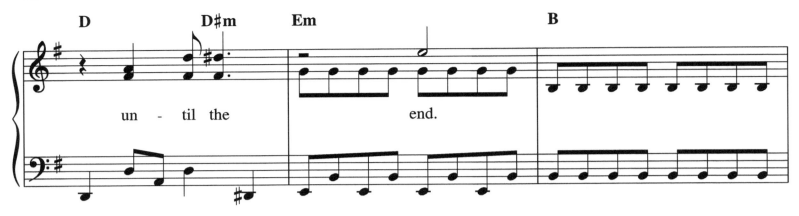

un - til the   end.

Can-cel my sub-scrip-tion to the   res - ur - rec - tion._

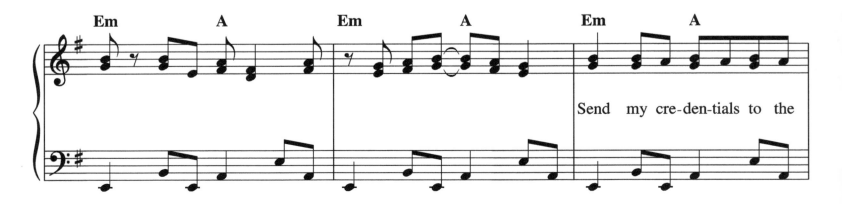

Send   my   cre-den-tials   to   the

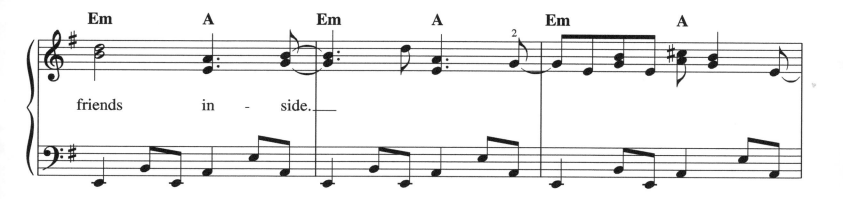

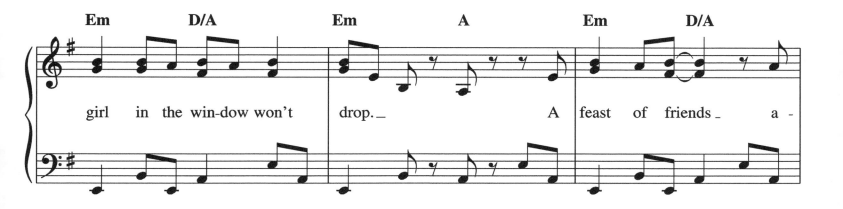

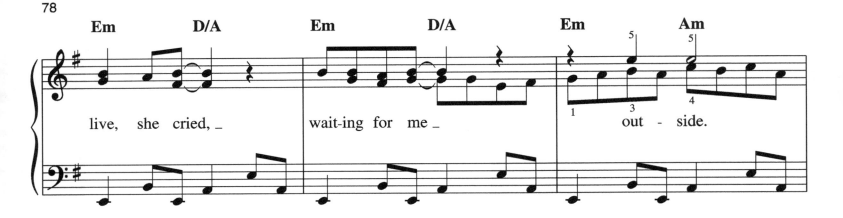

live, she cried, _ wait-ing for me _ out - side.

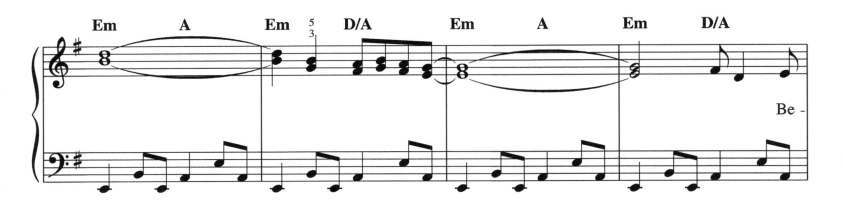

Be -

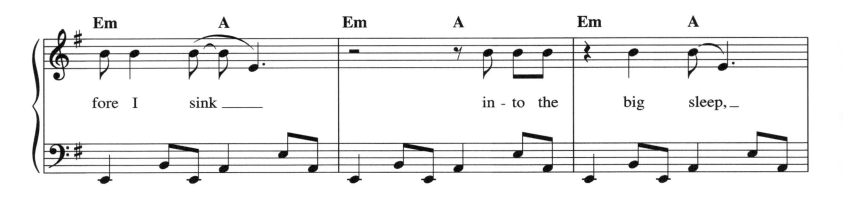

fore I sink _____ in - to the big sleep, _

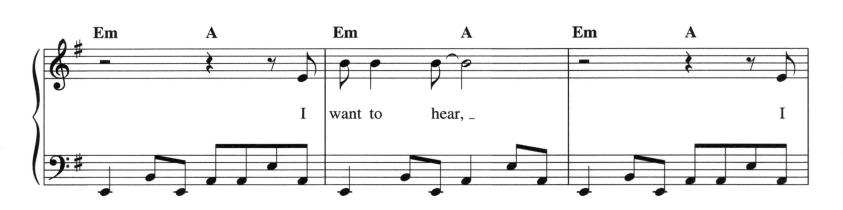

I want to hear, _ I

want to hear _ the scream of the

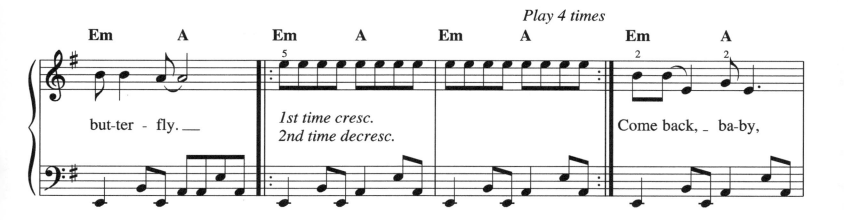

Play 4 times

but-ter - fly. _

1st time cresc.
2nd time decresc.

Come back, _ ba-by,

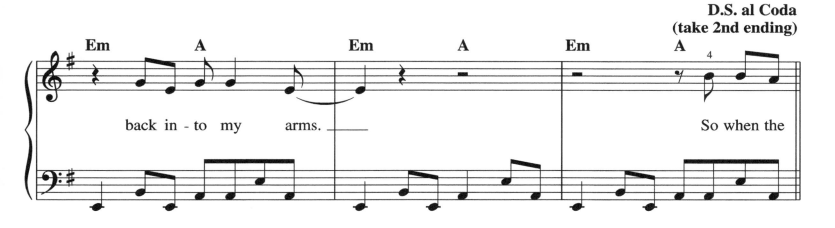

D.S. al Coda
(take 2nd ending)

back in - to my arms. _

So when the

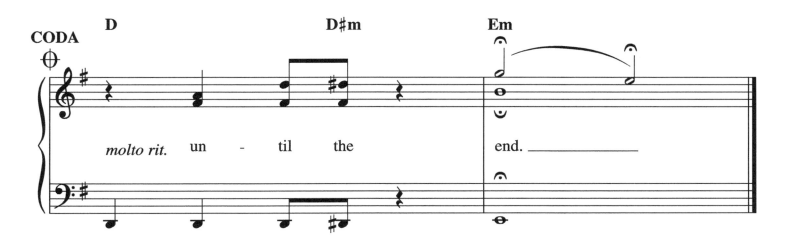

CODA

D   D♯m   Em

molto rit. un - til the end. _____

TOUCH ME

Words and Music by
THE DOORS

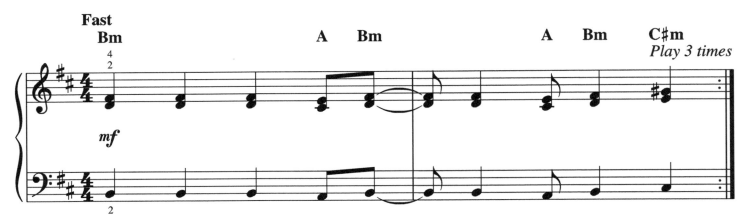

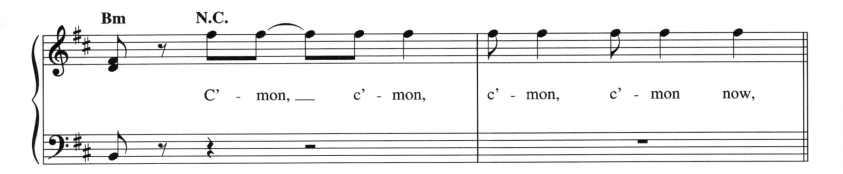

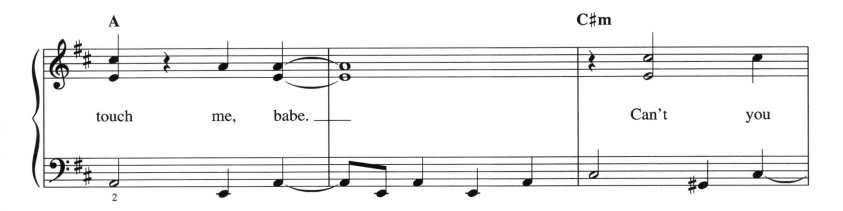

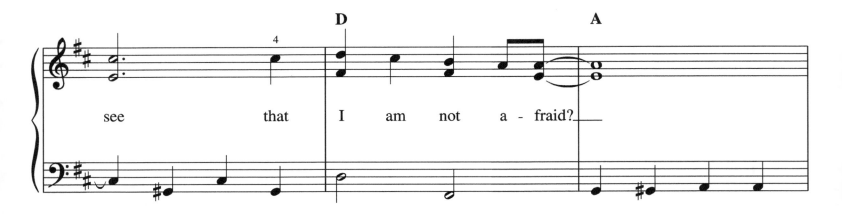

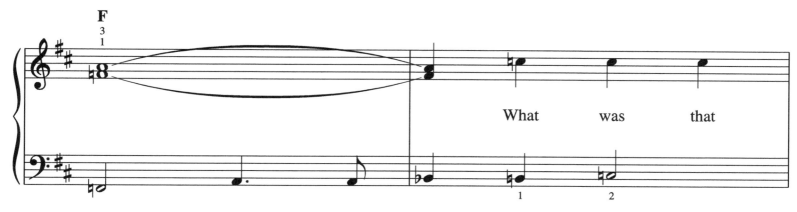

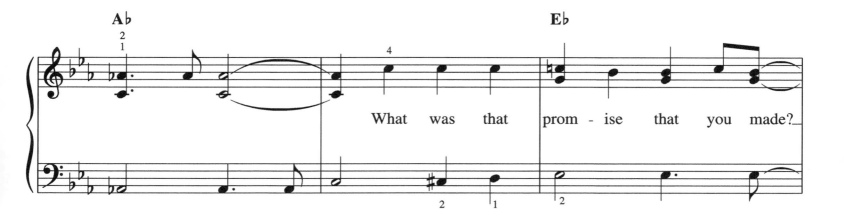

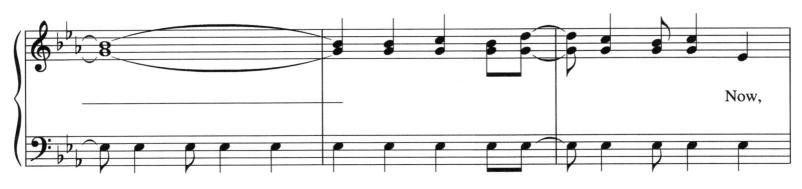

Now,

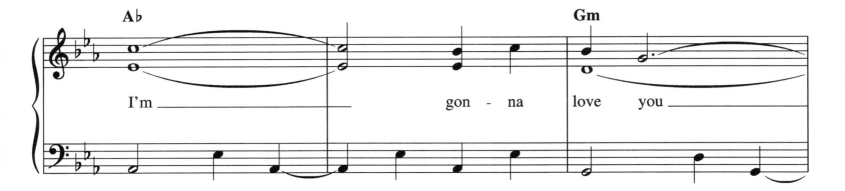

I'm ___ gon - na love you ___

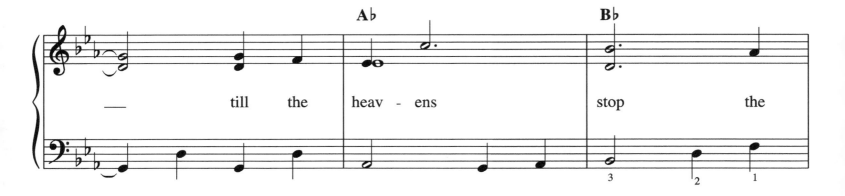

___ till the heav - ens stop the

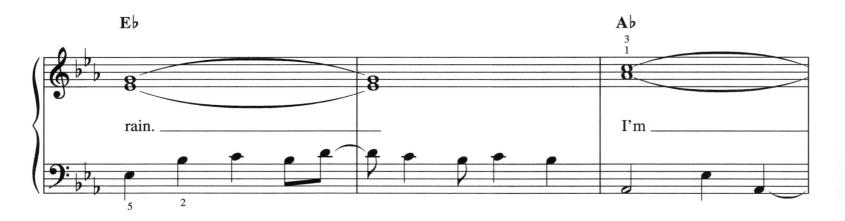

rain. ___ I'm

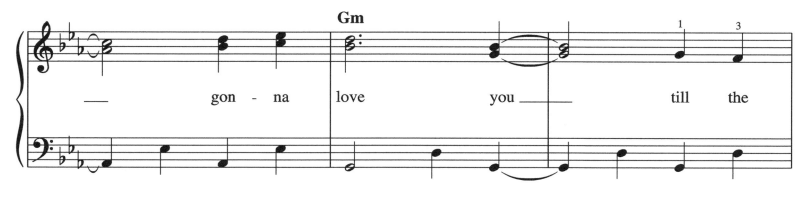

gon - na love you till the

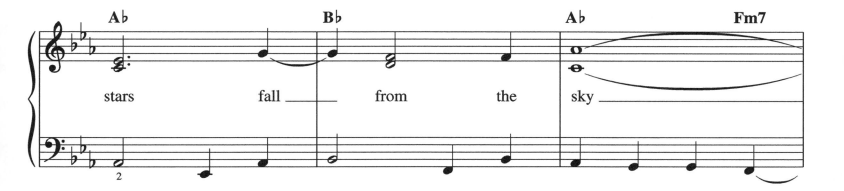

stars fall from the sky

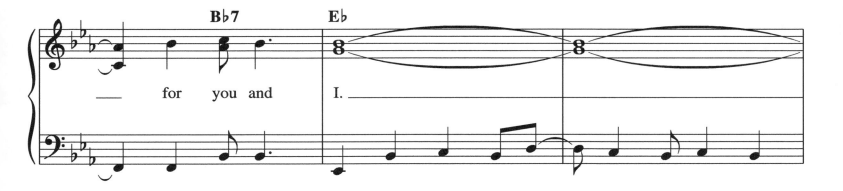

for you and I.

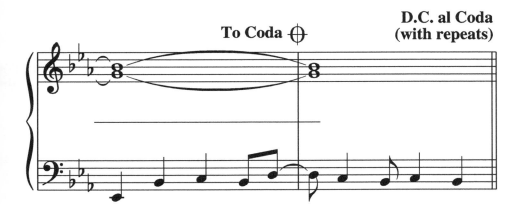

To Coda ⊕

D.C. al Coda
(with repeats)

CODA
⊕

A♭

I'm _____ gon - na love you _____

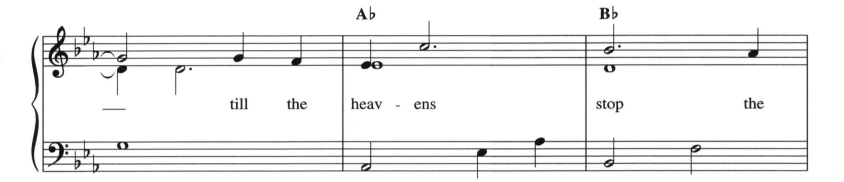

A♭ **B♭**

_____ till the heav - ens stop the

E♭ **A♭**

rain. _____ I'm _____

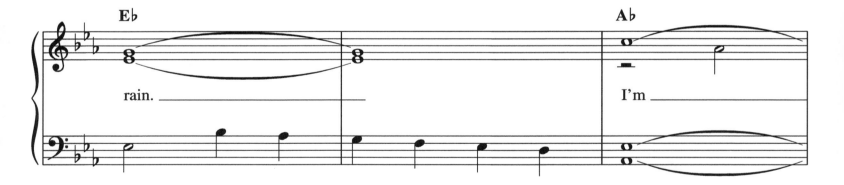

Gm

_____ gon - na love you _____ till the

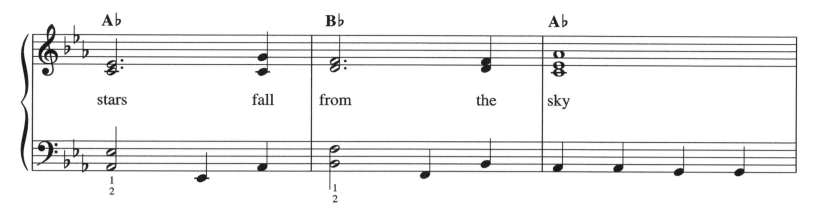

stars   fall   from   the   sky

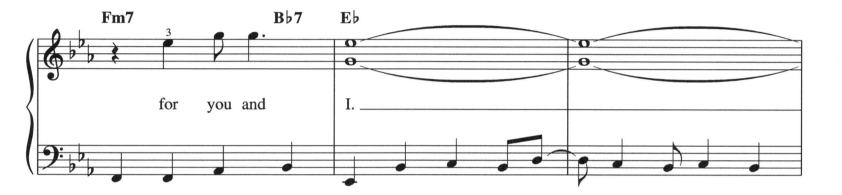

for   you and   I. _____

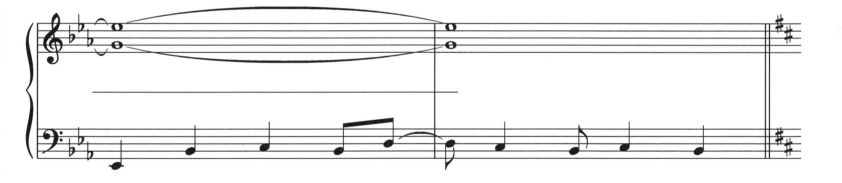

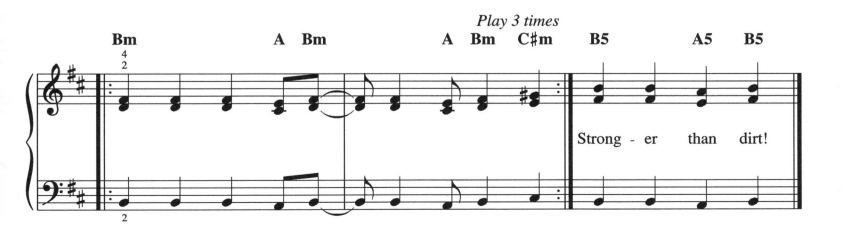

Play 3 times

Strong - er   than   dirt!

THE UNKNOWN SOLDIER

Words and Music by
THE DOORS

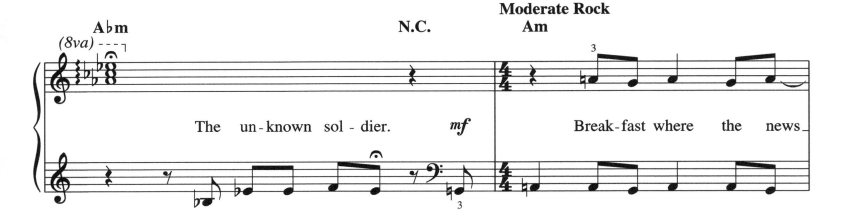

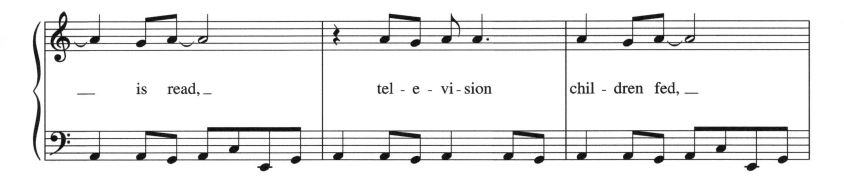

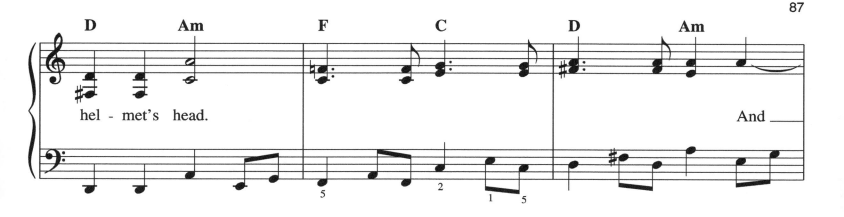

hel - met's head.　　　　　　　　　　　　And ___

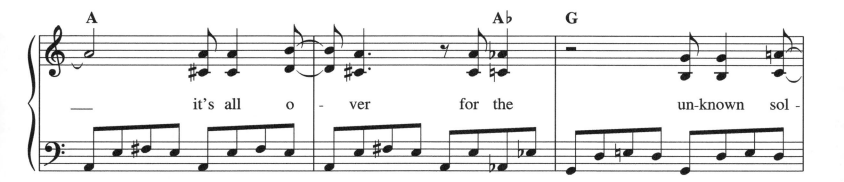

___　it's all o - ver　for the　　un-known sol -

- dier. _____　It's all o - ver　for the

un-known sol - dier, _____ uh　uh. _____

N.C.   *Play 6 times*

(Spoken:)   Company,

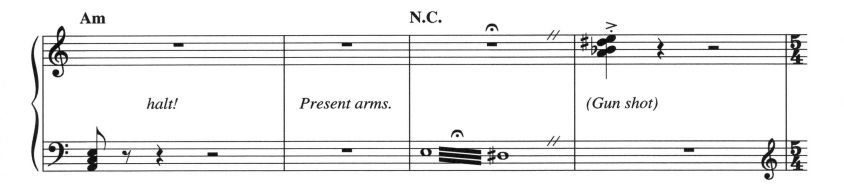

Am   N.C.

halt!   Present arms.   (Gun shot)

Slowly, mournfully
A♭m   G♭

(Sung:) Make a grave _ for the un-known sol-dier,   nes-tled in your hol-low shoul-der.

Moderate Rock
A♭m   G♭   F   C

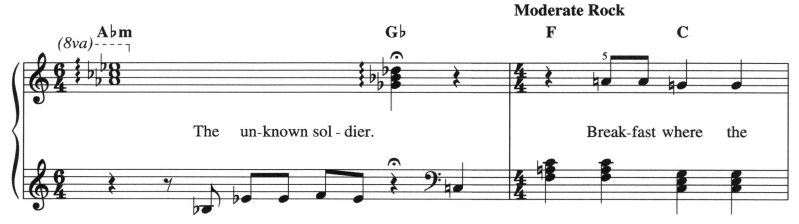

The   un-known sol - dier.   Break-fast where   the

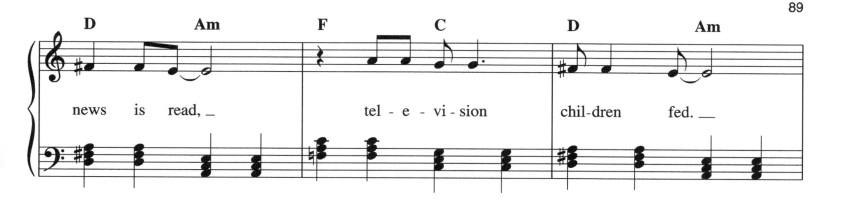

news is read, __ tel - e - vi - sion chil-dren fed. __

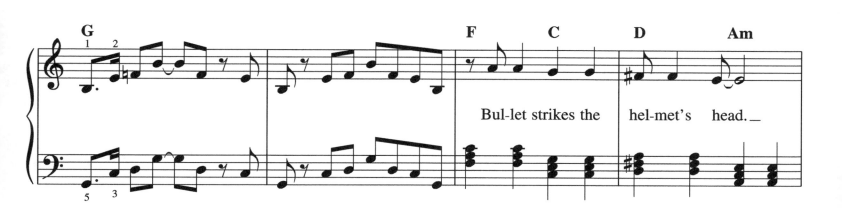

Bul-let strikes the hel-met's head. __

It's all o - ver.

The war is o - ver.

YOU MAKE ME REAL

Words and Music by
JIM MORRISON

Fast Blues

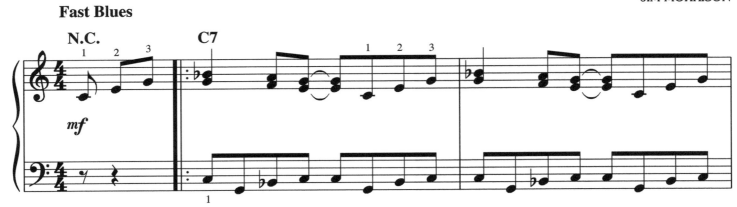

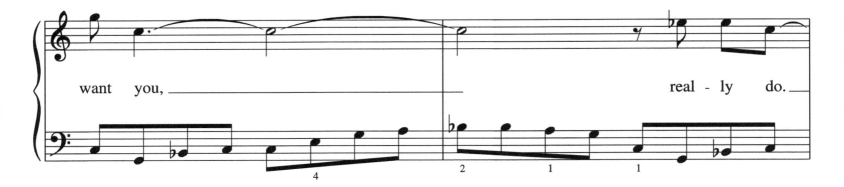

need you, ba - by,   {God   knows   I   do,__
                      {real - ly   do,__

'cause I'm   not

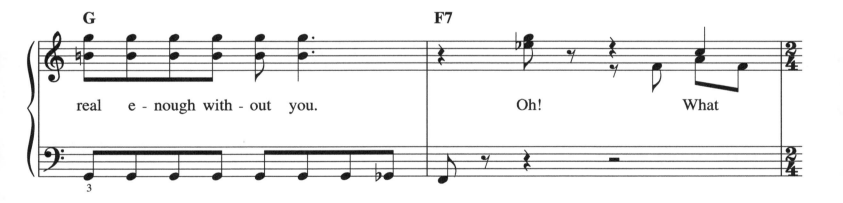

real   e - nough with - out   you.   Oh!   What

can   I   do?

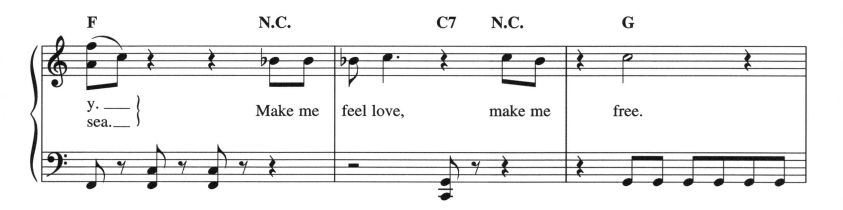

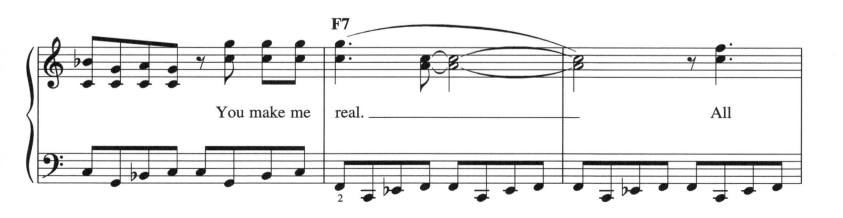

You make me real. _____ All

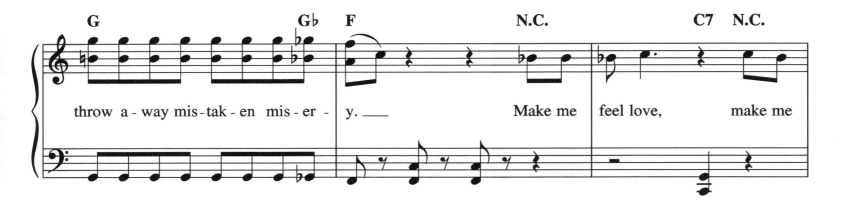

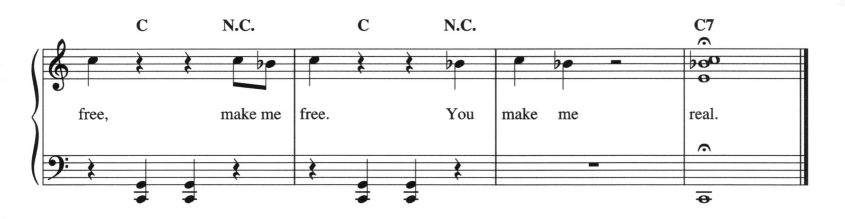